RUNNING OUT

The eye with which I see God is the same eye with which God sees me

Meister Eckhart
(c.1260–1327)

Running Out

DAVID HART

FIVE SEASONS PRESS · 2006

Published October 2006 by
Five Seasons Press
41 Green Street
Hereford HR1 2QH, UK

www.fiveseasonspress.com
books@fiveseasonspress.com

Distributed in USA by SPD
1341 Seventh Street, Berkeley CA 94710-1409
www.spdbooks.org

ISBN 0 947960 49 X

Designed & typeset
in Garamond Premier Pro Medium 11.5/14 pt
(except for the Baskerville epigraph, title &
dedication pages in honour of Birmingham)
at Five Seasons Press

and printed on
Five Seasons recycled paper
(*paper specification / polemic: page 272*)

by Cromwell Press
Trowbridge, Wiltshire, UK

For acknowledgements see Notes on page 265

Front cover based on an image by David Hart
who also produced the back cover montage
(using a photograph by Rebecca Farmer)

*Five Seasons acknowledges
financial assistance from*

for
Josh, Gabriel, Daniel,
Cressy & Caleb

CONTENTS

All Saints Elegies

Loving is good too, for love is hard

Rainer Maria Rilke

1.
I thought, if I arrange the musical instruments
in order in the field
the angels will come and play them,

and the angels did come and they
kicked the instruments and trod them
into the ground,

and they threw the instruments
into the bog, and they snapped the instruments
in pieces as if they were branches for a fire,

and the fire almost woke me,
almost brought me back
to begin again.

2.
They are called servants.
They are called to be servants.
They are called and they attend.

On another table some sheets partly written on
and discarded, here and there words, phrases,
here a whole line but written in such haste, —

A painting here of hills in twilight-stormlight,
a few notes in the words and an ironic cheer,
brief, distant, fading, loud again, brief, fading.

The translation must try to catch *servants*,
how they have the name,
how they are enlisted in the calling.

There was, I think, a great traveller known here,
beyond *here*, beyond *here*, yes, and further off.
'I want to go up that river.' Remember?

It's where she was born, she spoke that language,
she was patient, but cried out in spite of herself in her map
the name traveller, the actual word, *traveller*,

and then other names: *seaboard*, *edge*,
and here it says, 'I have raised a poem like a glass
in empty chorus

on the other side of the street,' and here
if I can make it out, 'behind the roses'.
Can you see the steps? The arguments?

Would this woman coming along now remember?
Or this one coming now?
Would this one?

3.
I thought, the white sheets are clear evidence
of the angels' presence, that they were here
offering themselves, that I had missed them.

The bloody marks on the sheets
might have been words, I mistook them for words.

Spread your wings, my loves, spread them wider
so that there is nothing but wings, nothing but,
nothing but, nothing but wings for as far as the,
for as far as the body can see, can see, can lose.
You see how I can talk, oh yes.

4.

My sigh speaks for me and I am my own doctor
of sigh, sigh claims me and I resist, I pause,
I consult sigh, I ask sigh now straightaway
what it wants, I tell sigh I am the (examine me)
doctor of sigh, sigh will not claim me, I shall be
ready for sigh. I sigh, I flow with sigh, I travel (look)
on the helter-skelter with sigh, I am the doctor of sigh, sigh
will not claim me. Sigh, I am in love with you (you),
you know me, sigh, you are beautiful. Sigh (will not)
will not claim me, I am the doctor of sigh,
sigh, take me over, do what you will with me,
sigh will not have me, I am the doctor (believe me)
of sigh, love me, sigh, O (sigh) love me.

5.

I thought, I will do the work of angels,
I will hold the pen, they will do the work,
and they came and stood around
and when I most wanted to hear clearly they
told loud obscene jokes and spoke in whispers,
and they ran around in circles
making fun of me. I stood my shaking ground,
the pen ready in my hand.
                              I thought,
if I am ready, they will do the rest,
I told myself this and if I didn't believe it
whose fault was that? I gave the angels so readily
their opportunity, I waited with my pen ready,
and they laughed at me, they kicked dust
that looked like words
into my notebook. I was, I knew then,
their plaything. A song was all I'd wanted,
the angels have so many, they could have (look at me)
spared me one, I waited with obvious longing, my pen
and my voice ready, I thought readiness
(what it really means as best intent, as best intent)
was what they wanted of me.

6.
A man is crossing the road and stops
because of something he can't quite grasp,
something inside him, something that is
asking him to pause, to wait a moment,
to be ready for something different that had
been there inside him secretly and now
needs to be heard clearly. So he stops and
the car horns spit and people through
car windows shout and swear at him
and lorries swerve to avoid him and buses
ease themselves around him, and the thought
if a thought it is—or it should be described
as something quite other—wedges
but doesn't show itself, won't become
explicit, until after an hour or more perhaps,
after seventy minutes perhaps,
seventy three minutes he is struck by an empty van
and is wounded so badly
his thought now.

7.
I thought, if the angels would like my life
they would have to wrench it from me, I would
put up an absurd fight, on my knees
I would fight them off. What to say on such a day
to represent thought, toes (you know toes)
dug deep in the earth? So much part of the earth
no dragging away from it would be possible,
angels would mistake me
for an icicle. Their eyes would be hurt (as science tells us)
by the sun burning back from the ice, me.
I would be my secret.

8.
Do you remember what you were about to say
that evening when you were interrupted,
that evening that would have been a different evening,
it was in your eyes but as yet inarticulately,
ready, I would say, ready, and you were indicating
with your eyes, ready, and with the whole readiness
of your body, ready, what was it, do you remember
what it was you were going to say?
                                                    The world,
I think you would agree, is a different place now.
What was it that evening you were about to say
when you were interrupted? Not that nakedness
would have come into fashion, what was it you were
about to say? The interruption was abrupt, your eyes
faded suddenly, they went grey, your mouth fell,
your body collapsed in on itself, so I think there was
something. What was it, what was it in that moment
that never came: you were going to say, what was it?

9.
Thought floats me, is tidal, roughs and slides me,
like a gull on the wind
but without a gull's mind,
and whether I am bold or shy I am taken by thought
to its caves,
to its cliff tops, to its flats and edges
as if it knows me, as if it craves something for me,
but on ledges
leaves me. Taunts the *I*
that is the maker of poems, slips *I* under its coat
for the next dark,
parades *I* for a moment
out of the dark, and lets go.

10.

I say to myself, what have you got under your coat?
And I reply, it's me under here, and I say to myself, prove it.
I walk along with my coat buttoned and the sun shining
until I say to myself again, prove it, go on, prove it's you
in there, but I pretend not to hear and I walk along
turning a corner, slipping behind a wall then along its cover
and into some trees. I am being followed, I hear the voice
again: Open your coat, prove it's you in there, is it you
in there? And I walk on, holding my coat closed, out now
into a yard and across the yard, hearing those footsteps
following me ready to say again: Prove it. So when I reach,
when I reach the river I stop and turn, I unhitch the buttons
of my coat and I open it, and I am not inside, I am only
the voice making the poem, and the coat
falls to the ground, anyone can (you can) have it.
And the voice moves on, free now, no questions
left to ask, no demands
to be met, through the river, up the other bank,
across the meadow and into the city,
out of the invisible audible faintly.

11.

Thought can issue a ticket to an angel,
can wait in the field at the kissing gate
at the ecstatic time when the tide
as it can never have done before comes
these hundred miles up the river
in its bare feet kicking the flow inwards—
look at the picnic now, and the gate a broken raft
in a fold of the answer. Thought has done this.

13.

Thought by itself doesn't. You see how it stops before.
No apples. An angel waits to be introduced
without conditions. Thought's palpitations. The edge
of the cliff and no view, nothing there. I want you to
gather round and. The Lord in his. I am, choking on,
before you start, check. This is what we'll do.

A hand comes pushing aside the stars, parting the planets,
it has stretched right through the galaxies, from the edge
but I pretend I can't see or think *edge*, it comes
snapping through thought, it releases a
wash that floods back to *edge*
but I pretend I can't see or think *edge*, and it touches me
the way a light 'Excuse me' touches, on my sleeve.
You, you, you, please, you, sit down at the piano
and play this for me. Let me hear it as it might be,
as it might have been, as it can never be except.
The piano stool is empty, the keyboard is closed, the notes
are inside, locked in. Please, you, you, you,
please, you, unlock it, sit down, play this for me?

14.
Here he is again with the theme of the edge.
Angels will risk it if he will. They will come and stand
on one leg on the edge of *edge* if he will.
He says he knows *edge* is *edge* is *edge*,
but as for the edge of *edge* has he ever known it?

Here he is again with the theme of the edge.
What can be seen but pure horizon? It hurts but (but)
is manageable. What can be seen but ocean? From here
it is a beautiful. View. Look, mountains and beyond them
more. Mountains. Without edges, only gradual slopes.

Here he is again with the theme of the edge.
The edge is in eyes and it hurts. Eyes have deep in them
edge and the thought of the edge of *edge*, and it hurts.
Look into the eyes, see *edge*, see the thought of the (the)
edge of *edge*, let the hurt hurt, he says, he says,
and again he says it, look into the eyes of *edge*
and let them hurt. Let the edge of *edge* appear now.

Here he is again with the theme of the edge.
He thinks there may be more yet to be said
about *edge* and the edge of *edge*. He pauses,
he continues, he pauses again, he continues again,

and *edge* is here, look, it is here, and there further out
is the edge of *edge*. There is a ladder. There is (is)
a ladder leaning against nothing at all, the words
will do whatever needs to be done. So far (shivering)
then no further than this or that *edge* is. Like this.

15.
I meet thought coming towards me through waves,
I stand here on the shore meeting thought
looking ridiculous as the tide comes
and goes, comes and goes, and me in my thin coat.

I tell thought this is a farce
and I tell thought to rummage in itself again.
'Rediscover yourself,' I say, casually (casually),
even turning away. But thought grabs me,
has me round the throat, will easily
throttle me. But a boatman passing
hits thought with an oar, concussing thought,
leaving thought laid out on the sand.

I wave to the boatman as he rows away,
he waves with a puzzled look back at me.

16.
Everything is in hiding.
Hiding can be smelt here.
Everything is in hiding, every thing we are
everything that is, is in hiding, trying (as we say, *trying*)
to get away, can't you smell—do I mean *smell*?—wheedle—
the secretion of it, like a fire
lit with seaweed fresh from the ocean
and put out with flames from a volcano,
and the angels are watching, their absence present,
can't you smell that, and nothing else? Nothing.
Hiding is what is wanted, was longed for, is what we've got.

17.
Thought
lay at the side of the road and waited and couldn't wait,
and is waiting and can't wait. The road itself
disintegrates, thought has no road to travel on, on which
to stumble more, has no road to fall from, there is no
road now on which to stumble or to fall from. Shall we (we)
have tea, shall we invite God to tea, and his angels,
bring out the apple cake, the gritty macaroons,
put on a CD—the Mozart Requiem—cry?

18.
There is everything to say and nothing to say,
starting from the red carnations and the dog daisies
and the maidenhair fern, everything and nothing,
starting from the tea trolley today without biscuits,
starting from the well-trodden carpet,
starting from the chairs with the padded backs,
starting from the stories told until they no longer hurt
and hurt more than ever, starting from the drifting eyes
and the eyes alight precisely now (now) with what is possible,
starting from the missing years, from the plastic table top,
from the notice board with notices hanging off it, starting from
the loud bang deep in the chest which may be a smile,
starting from 'in here' and 'out there', from every-nothing,

starting from the earthquake somewhere else on the
                    (sshhh) planet,
starting from whatever round it is of the FA Cup,
starting from the books on the shelves around the room,
                    on the circular table,
starting from an oasis in the Sahara when no one is there,
starting from the moon over Burma, over Birmingham,
over Belize, over Botswana, over Borth, over Barmouth,
over Bournemouth, over Bridgend, over Bradford, over Bali,
                    the mouth around it.

How to run everything and nothing to ground?
How to locate it and brush it into the pan?

19.

Someone is pleased about something and the fire warms them,
they eat now from a warmed plate and the ceiling is white,
they go outside and feel the chill in the night air,
they hear an animal in the distance in its—
      caught, lamed, in a corner it hasn't known before—
           pain,
and the inside of the room is warm again
and quiet, except for the wind getting up and the (pain)
pain in the wind against the small, cherished, ancient window.
Someone remembers they have been pleased today,
they remember they ate from a warmed plate under a white ceiling,
they will remember again how good it was to eat,
they will remember again the warm room,
they will remember the white ceiling,
and they will remember the animal crying out (out there) its
           pain.
      Thought can do much more than this,
      thought can do amazing things.

20.

Bring the cart to the back gate, won't you,
don't make any fuss, do it decently but crabwise,
and without comprehension, don't pretend (my friend)
you know what you're doing, take the money.
      One of these days
I must take the *somebody* exam,
I must work hard in preparation for it,
I must apply my self diligently and with a
      grim (bright, cheerful) look, I must sit
and do it, get it done,
the *somebody* exam passed, at last.

21.

Now I am going to walk around thought
where the path used to be, now I shall walk
where the valley used to meet the mountain,
now I am going to walk where the flowers
used to be, where in their season once they
flourished, now I am going to walk
where the small animals used to be, in and out
of the hedges, now I am going to walk where
the air made me sing, now I am going to walk
where thought was once.
                    This cramped song now
is choking, it is confined, the walk is off, the walk
will not happen, the poem's walk is around
and around confined. It drags me along
by my tongue around and around, around and around
and we have this conversation: 'Thought was here,
I do believe thought was here,' 'No, over this way a little,
thought was over here,' 'But I remember clearly,'
'No, *I* remember clearly,', and so the poem and I
come to no agreement, except tiredness, except—
how to say it?—except by attempting a calm retreat
from wherever
thought was. By the book.

22.

Wind and rain and dark knowing will perform (perform),
I shall be their audience (audience),
I shall *thank my lucky stars*, I shall will myself
as audience into action. But be warned, wind and rain and dark,
there may come a time when (*when*)
I as audience shall present myself at my starkest but
not tonight,
perhaps not tonight.

23.
Here is an angel scratching its head
trying to think what a head is for

on the roof of the world puzzling about
what a head is for,

                    and suddenly remembers

and there is such a cry of pain
the whole world shakes. *My God,*
stop the world shaking, stop it, stop it!

Then thought in the angel's sore head
becomes composed into a rhythm
and the angel is away again, flying.

I am waiting in the grove of trees,
without knowing how I am waiting,

and hours later I am still waiting
without knowing how I am waiting,

and days and years later I am still waiting
without knowing how I am waiting,

because that angel had looked me in the eye
out of its sore head, and I had looked away.

Shall we play souls and angels?
Shall we play that game now?
Shall we get the game going
and see what unhappens?

24.
When we are taken by the hand,
                what is it that takes us?
When we are taken by the hand,
                what is it that is taken?

25.

Thought comes claiming its reward
and finds itself adrift on a flooded river,
and look, the angel who caused the flood,
is running now just ahead of it, leading it on.
And thought still doesn't know what is happening,
thought doesn't know it is adrift on the flood,
still it awaits its reward, still grinning it awaits
its pat on the back, as the flood takes it,
as the angel draws the flood on, just ahead of it,
thought—independent, thorough, exact—rides on,
is here for the ride, believes the ride is taking it
on a celebratory journey to the award ceremony,
and the angel just out of sight
leads the flood on, wide-widens it, deep-deepens it,
leads it on.

26.1

Inside, I want to say something,
inside, I need to say something,
and if what I say merely floats away
or is thrown back at me
nothing will have changed
except for the slight noise and being stuck
with the rootless pain of it,
my guts will be floating loose
in the hole, *that* will be my place still.
But if I am heard, really heard,
something will be newly lit.
Being heard will hurt,
being lit will hurt,
being loved will hurt,
and oh I want that, I want that,
and I can't bear it, I can't, I can't!

26.2
Does it matter what name is given to my calling out,
I could name it *calling out*, I could name it *shout, yell,*
name it *crying out*, name it *sobbing of my heart,*
howl might best say it, I could name it *scream.*
I could name it *quiet disintegration*, I could name it
slow dislocation of myself from myself, the angel holds
open the door, the Holy One's light is like no other

and I am only further out, even the far filter of it
          that reaches me
makes me step back, and back and back.

32.
I come running without running,
I come running without running,
look, I come running without running
until I don't arrive.
          What would I have sung?
Something drove me to run without running,
  what was that?
Something drove me to run without running,
look, something drove me to run without running
until I failed to arrive.
          What would I have sung?
The activity must have wearied me,
running without running must have worn me out,
running without running must have worn me out
so I failed to arrive.
          What would have been my first note,
what would have been the next
and the next
and the next, until what I would have heard
  myself making
would have been song?

33.
The body is tidal,
it is not containable,
it can be rushed towards the open-armed shore
and heaved back somersaulting
into the ocean. I know now.

Towards the line

—one—

A dance in two seasons

I saw you first on that long, frail summer evening,
eating little at the picnic
but sliding away to turn and swirl and circumvent
quietly alone. Some bold, private writing
was done then. Nor have you ever spoken to me
except to whisper, *Describe the grasses.*
I have seen the deep cut graves on the cliff top.
The whole cliff is open-mouthed skull,
the whole world is skull and the whole world's heart
is in its bloody mouth. Between trees moving so freely
as barely to be seen at all you laugh, beautifully.

I see you now in what seems to be Winter,
seed-pods lie broken open and crusty on the ground,
you walk hardly protected against the wind
biting into an apple you've picked from the sack
seeming to hide behind each beech and oak. Slower,
shrivelled, impossible writing must be done
under siege. I hear you wanting to speak to me
but no words come. Bone after bone
tries to reflect the grey say of your body.
I have seen the sky taking its cut of us,
the whole sky believing itself finite
around us as if to grasp and squeeze us.
Between trees holding their ground in the light
of a billion years you ask nothing but wait,
laughing mournfully.

On Athos: in the café at Daphni

I tell myself, sitting with my notebook
in the café at Daphni,
I shall collect evidence. I tell myself
sitting quietly
as I sip my coffee, enjoying every private
lip of its tip, every soft
promise and float of heat, if I can
collect cold,
hard evidence—I mean words—
so as to know. I need a decision and ask
for more coffee, I say, *Please*
blacker and thicker than before, please,
more strength in it, more depth of sip, more
cling of tip, more—and I flounder. 'Of quiet,'
the man says. *Yes*, I say,
of quiet, coffee strong with quiet, and,
waiting now,
holding back the rush of the world, I continue
in myself
the accumulation of evidence:
must have contact prints of words,
must have a sequence of words in minor chords.

'It will be up the steps then,' the man says,
'without counting them,
on your knees then without counting the hours,
enjoying then the gift of thin soup
without murmur, afterwards to reach, hold,
wait, yield, whisper, hold,
wait,' he says, 'open
as waiting will the hearts
of the cockroaches
in your blood.'

Someone far away asks, 'Will there be
luminous, elastic, convincing music?' There is
an awkwardness, my plan
is washed out the way a painting

of the beloved
disappears in rain. I am awash impulsively with
sanctuary hunger, losing my way who
can swim
only a little, only biliously, like a maimed
gull rising and falling at the will
of the lovely waves, so
when my coffee comes I take it aside
and spit in it. The man

begins to sing
the *kontakion* of the day, but how
will death

be possible without evidence that I can
hear what matters
at the roll-call of the *anaphora* sung
and sung again, how will I see
without digital photos secretly the *iconostasis*
and its doors opening, how hear
without stumbling on a waymarked path,
how kneel without The Guide
To The Sacred Mountain, how to know
what I have known always?

Her name was Olwen

Her name was Olwen free as a bird,
drifter, found the absurd
in our routine, spoke a long line
I would begin to dance to, on my own
with the memory. In those days
I was fitter, sang on Sundays the praise
of the Almighty, eyes in the book
some of the time, but a sore lack
of get-up-and-go kept me in the village
so that Olwen was merely a spillage
of gossip, long gone from me
into I didn't know what kind of sea
of knowing and being and wondering
and here I was still singing
but in the bath and in the fields up Bryn Coch
where Mrs Lewis—How are you then, bach?—
and me forty-one going on fifty
would stumble in my throat and say,
It's a funny life, thinking it's not funny at all,
thinking what Olwen would say, To hell
with funny, it's really crazy
so why didn't you marry me? Because the lie
of this land was against me.
Against you, she'd say, away
and out of it to Paris first she went, sent
me one postcard, the Seine cut out and twisted
and stuck back on and no message only,
Think of me in every city on the map
till I find my love. I couldn't even rip it up
but have it still, to gaze at, to go over and over
what might have been, put my lips
to her name. Olwen, I say, perhaps,
and go to bed every night with that ache.
Mrs Lewis sees, I'm sure in my eyes, forsake
that woman long gone, here's a widow
who likes you.

I'd like you to know
For Meredith Andrea

I'd like you to know
in Sutton Park today a bit of grit
got into my sandal. Also

I helped a ladybird
on Selly Oak station.

I have thought more about the pain
likely for a writer of poems.
You'd like to know this, perhaps.

I came out of Wyndley baths
wondering if I might find humous
and oat cakes in a shop here.

I remember there is something life-giving
about laughter by a lake.
No one here tells me there are
pipistrelle bats.

Alice Oswald won't, I dare say,
abandon Devon for the Second City.
We will have to write our own
                    exasperated ripples our
                    strenuous glitter-reeds our
                    palliative popping alleluias our
                    calculation of accidentals made by our
                    little river—

In the corner shop supermarket just out of the park
presided over by an elderly Indian woman
by means of a few words, gesture and calculator
and sometimes a smile
I find Ryvita and Cheddar slices. I deny myself
the Royal Edinburgh Shortcake. And I

suppose perhaps
you wouldn't know Welsh hymn singing
is good for crying of an afternoon at home alone
one's heart out.

Soup of the day
At the Dean Gallery, Edinburgh

I'll have the soup of the day, please—
courgette, mozzarella, *etcetera*—
and a pot of tea. I'll feel warmed

to return to Picabia, to Duchamp, to Magritte
and to Breton and to Ernst
who played their dreams
on squirrels' teeth.

I am glad they are here but I hope I am
not being tricked. I know the uniforms suspect me,
making me carry my bag in my hand—
'Not on your back, Sir, security.'

'You won't, will you,' I shall say,
'prod me towards a side door
that leads out there—what a lovely sunny day it is!—
to the trucks. You won't
order me to undress, I won't have to try to
leave my soul clandestinely
with Man Ray. Will I have to share a truck
with all those other Surrealist aficionados—We are

a sophisticated people. If there is to be gas let it be
a fun canister, painted in bangles of primary colours
with a little turquoise
for the play-smoke. Hallucination
is such a delight.'
                    I have bought the book,
I'm looking forward to going home—flying, really—
to my own bed.

The smell of death

i.m. Alfred James Hart

The smell of death is piss. My father's, for instance,
way back now who every working day
and sometimes into the night
sucked up other people's into a pipette for testing,

lying on the floor outside the bathroom gone.
What was his last thought, in his head the last burn?
After a week of headaches, in the bathroom then, a fit man,
what was his last thought-flicker?

And the last thing he was aware of touching:
water, sink, towel, his ear, the door, the floor?

No more taking the dog for a walk,
pissing in a hedge,
coming back for tea.

Repeats

Casablanca will be repeated again and again long after I'm gone.
At my funeral someone might say, 'It was a long haul,'
and not hear themselves using a metaphor, and I won't hear it.

The plane will take off again and again with her without him.
Someone will sit at the table almost in the corner of the tea room
near the painting of longing on a Welsh quay and write a poem.

As things are now I can find a map—look: north of Marrakesh,
down from Tangier, get on the Internet, consult a Travel Agent.
Leave this poem for someone to say: *Line lengths not quite right.*

I could put a note in my will: leave the TV on, let the old films roll,
it'll keep me here unseen, in my room in my house, the postman
will remember, *He lives here, he must be in, watching Casablanca.*

All day and all night the drama will be told, at tables, at the piano,
the risks, the tense encounters, what must happen, what doesn't.
Someone in a room somewhere might say, *He'd have enjoyed this.*

Bogart, Bergman and Rains will live until the planet burns out,
over and over the joys, the pain, the chance meeting, the wrench,
and me dust, words flaked, me earth-recycled, eyes and ears gone.

Mr Amichai

The world is full of people who are going to die, Mr Amichai,
and your turn has come. A blessing I ask then
on your after-death journey, a blessing I ask on your memory,
a *Thank you,* too, a confused thank you, an it's-all-done thank you,

and I see you smiling and frowning at this:
you've written all your poems now, and I'm adding this one,
and you are saying, 'It's not necessary, it's not a good idea at all,
go and enjoy yourself, go for a walk,
talk to the absence, be ready for a surprise,
ask a blessing on all children,
don't hold me up with a poem, let me go.'

And even as I'm working on this poem, R.S., too, has gone.
Did you ever meet, did you read each other's poems?
You can travel together, two old poets of uncertain temper,
Jew and Christian priest,
Jerusalem and Jerusalem-translated-into-Wales.

If you do look back, if you will, bless us ambivalently, strangerize us,
in the world still, writing still, still attending workshops,
still thinking of our reputations, still trying to get it right, not yet dead,
not yet taken by the sharp wind.

Walking the streets of the boarded-up world

Walking the streets of the boarded-up world I rehearse to myself
the frail fragments that are becoming my *Walking the streets* poem.

As I walk the streets in the bright lights of the disarming world
the frail fragments of my *Walking the streets* poem begin to emerge.

Rehearsing the frail fragments of my *Walking the streets* poem
I walk the streets this way and that of the veiled, padlocked world.

As I stand on a corner a young man in a moving car having prepared
a gob full of spit spits it out at me, aiming it at my face accurately.

All of them in the car congratulate themselves with loud laughter
on a job well done. I stare after them confused wiping myself down.

I have been well spat on as I walk the streets of the boarded-up world
listening for what will become my *Walking the streets* poem,
I am in the streets wiping from my face a gob of well-aimed spit.

No one else it seems saw what happened, it was my private secret,
the men in the car congratulated themselves as they drove away.

Walking the streets of the world we are born to rehearsing my poem,
the fragments, the loose phrases and wild, hurt words form themselves.

As I walk the streets in the bright lights of the open-armed world
the frail fragments of my *Walking the streets* poem begin to emerge.

Why did Christ as I walked working on my fragments spit at me?
Why with this sudden anointing has he entertained and loved me?

I live in David's house

I live in David's house, it's a bit of a mess,
so many books and paper and whatever else
has been kept vaguely with intent, the delusions
will need a big removal van and lots of boxes.

The garden, too, had good purpose and some care
back there in those optimistic summers,
covered in high growth again now of thistles, ferns,
long grass, what's left of a Japanese shrub.
One of the plastic chairs in the yard
blew over recently and he stood it up again,
so he does notice.

This morning in a charity shop I bought
Scenic Wonders: Exploring Britain,
it's been a while now since he was over there
in Wales, crossing marsh in the hills,
light-headed by the sea, along the cliff path. I thought
here in the book are the Swallow Falls, here's Cader Idris,
here's Saint Govan's Head, he'll like that.

He is restless,
he is here and not here,
I keep up with him easily sometimes
then I lose him,
I don't know what he wants or, more to the point,
what he's doing about getting it
or allowing it. I watch and wait,

living here
pogger by pogger,
email by email,
poem by poem,
sigh by sigh,
knowing there's something else
if I could get his attention.

Don't bark at me
Aberystwyth, 1950s; Shropshire, February 2000

Don't bark at me, cat,
it can't be as strange as that,
the givenness.
                         The fishing boats that went out in the bay
            brought back no oranges,
            and I never heard anyone say
            the sea had no right
            to fly up over the promenade
            and break down walls
            and flood the streets.
                                    Nasal sprays
        were not used for knees, pessaries
        were not used for eyes, poultices
        were not prepared to be eaten.

In my father's laboratory I learned to pipette urine samples
and to read the signs, I learned
that we have different bloods
and that they need matching.

Don't bite me, snowdrops,
  it can't be as strange as that,
  the givenness.
                          The sun that went down over the bay
didn't burn the sky away.
                        Analgesics
      were not for watering the flowers, emetics
      were not for picnics, expectorants
      were not given out in church.

In my father's laboratory I learned the work of white coats,
that ice cream could carry typhoid,
and what guinea pigs were used for.
                                    The battleship
            didn't anchor in the bay
            after merely playing at war
            but all I smelt then on its deck
            was the salty metal.

Poetry
was the curfew tolling the knell of parting day
and Welsh was the language of the angels,
puritanical ones, upright, orderly.
                              Potatoes
  were not handed out for the school photo, broken biscuits
  were not given out in assembly,
    the crates of milk didn't come from cormorants.

From my father's on-call work I knew of the boy
broken by the bus,
pulled out dying from underneath it
by his father crying.
                    This was order,
                    these were the rules.

This is how it was

For Fred Davies

This is how it was, I said, a long time ago
when I lived in Heol Nanteos in Penparcau next door
to the man who played outside left for Aberystwyth Town,
and Fred had the name then on the tip of his brain
and soon came up with 'Teddy Thomas'
and I said, 'There was a tall dark centre forward,'
and Fred said 'Eddie Ellis' and started to name then
the whole team: Teddy Bevan, Stuart Griffiths,
Gareth Hopkins, Jackie Johnson . . .

I said I sang in the St Michael's church choir
and Fred said he did, too—about four or five years
before me—W.R. Allen the choirmaster 'was strict' but I said
I remembered him as benign.
'Remember Ernie Morgan, the Wintle brothers,
Michael Lewis—big in music in America now, he is,'
and when the name clicked into place I said,
'I was an altar server with him at St Anne's, Penparcau.'
'Remember we got paid 6d for funerals and weddings?
And we had to take our surplice home to be washed.'

I'd not remembered the names of the boats:
Pride of the Midlands (owned by Ben White),
City of Birmingham ('Spanny')—
and me now most of my life in that city—

and I said I carried the Scout flag
in the Remembrance Day procession, Fred said he played
in the British Legion band, and so did
Will Nell in the Workhouse (where Bronglais now is,
and a part of the old building still used),
'and do you remember Happy Agnes with her shopping trolley?'

I didn't, but when we got on to Ardwyn School
a mixed bag of memories: Mr Ellis the Headmaster—
two Mr Ellises one after the other?—Roy James, Mr Beynon,
Mrs—or was it Miss?—Mainwairing . . .
Oh some of that still hurts.

I said I remember playing marbles in the gutter with Dai Young,
and in the yard of his father's garage—'Gwalia,' said Fred,

'below the Infirmary,' I said (where my father worked),
and in between where I went to junior school, North Road,
all three gone now: Hospital, School, Garage,
and not a gutter these days you could play marbles in.

Chapels are closing, too. One, Fred tells me, is a pub,
but the singing continues. Fred sings and with the local choir
has sung in Toronto, Stratford (Ontario),
Salt Lake City, San Francisco, Brittany, Cologne . . .

This is a poem you, reader, perhaps, can continue,
the poem me and Fred began, with a chance meeting.

Work, the work

*Beethoven rose at daybreak, no matter what the season,
and went at once to his work-table*

Anton Schindler

"**IF I** COULD FALL out of bed—
If I could fall—
If I could contrive a fall—
If I could fall out, crawl to the table, put the pen to work,—

Not enough is yet abandoned—

Not enough is yet abandoned something clings—

Not enough—I have been taken to

    bleak corners of sanctuary,
    the Voice Out Of Silence imprisoned me
    to use my pain,
    I am bound-bait
    for what has not yet been caught. My brother
    who had no brother lived six days,
    did not know me, was not me, might have been me, was not

to be taught by Rovantini, Koch, Pfeifer and Neefe,
to hear the work, the work of Hiller, Benda, Grétry and Paisello,
did not live to know his own name, my name. Lived
only six days, was not to inherit
Pergolesi, Bach, Handel, Mozart and Haydn,
was not to exercise the violin, viola, organ and klavier,
was not to stomach Rossini excellent fluffmaster,
was not to see Vienna, was not to compose or direct,
did not live to know his own name, my name.
was not to hide from Napoleon's cannon,
was not to be daily heart-broken,
was never to piss in a pot. I have his name, he no longer needed it
so I had it. I have not solicited

    the fruits of my baptism. Alone
    I have limped initiate through undergrowth a wounded stoat,
    I have stumbled about the cemetery competing for *Adoramus te,*
    I was heard testing *Et in terra pax* on a dog—
    a woman threw down flowers and ran—
    I worked my arguments in secret, discord
offered no apology to chord,

nor interruption to flow for breakages,
nor shout to pianissimo for corruscation,
nor minor to major for grief,
nor fugue to cadence for the chase, revealed to me
at the shrill warp of an age, at the dangerous edge
where dizziness—
                            On my favourite for-silence seat in the forest
asleep into dream a finger out of heaven finding my throat
I composed
the whole Solemn Mass. I woke
to find my notebook off my lap into mud
and a dog pissing against my leg *legato espressivo*. Who will lick my

stomach clean? My joints loose? My eyes clear? Who will
unblock my ears?! I am bled of sound, scourged with swollen feet,
jaundice, dropsy, hepatitic cirrhosis, an opened soul
and
I must dance the breach-dance and dance it quick—dear Czerny
believing in me, my asymmetricks, disconvention, improprietous
drifting.   Where was I?
                            Near the Archduke's

a policeman his look an arm-lock
arrested me for vagrancy, spooned me away sour honey.
I saw a man with no arms in an empty room
attempting to make a fortepiano from chair legs.
                                          Did I imagine the kiss,

did Antonie give me only half a case of—Begin again:
For all my presence,   her illness,   my playing—Begin again:
I assigned affection, my open-wound-soul—Begin again:
No shagfest then. In sleek silk with lowered eyes,—
Only gut-wrench, throat-winch, *van Ill-begotten* will bring disrepute,
Bait-brute-will bite, get him out!
        In her house plenty of lace napkins.
        A chaffinch in a cage, dirge-bright-hymn.
        A staircase wide enough for six horses.
        Crystal chandeliers enough to confuse the seraphim,
I am ill-begotten, woe-begotten—Begin again:

scrounging towards cadence, *van Woe-begotten, Limping Brute,*
mere Heavenbait, shoved
into grief-light-grafting, heaven-bearing,—Begin again:

      Ill-begotten, woe-begotten—
      I, *Fate-heavy fan Bloat-hoofy*
      fin Bait-heaving glum Brute-hooven
at the fortepiano *Bleat-heaving bait-heavy beat-heaving.* I am
Bleat-hum-hymn Bait-bleating Earwig Loudwig van Brute-heaving
      Lewdwag BLEAT-HEAVY van Rude,
      in the ditch *BLOAT-HEAVING Herr van*
      Loudwig BRUTE-HEAVENING in ditch-scent-hum
      Bait-heaving *VOLCANIC RUNT*
      open to the infecting chill. Some bastard

called *Beethoven*
filched my leaked ink,
stood behind me copy-swabbing, pilfer-teasing. It was *him,*
he nicked my name, traded my peace
for a place in the queue,—   That arch-swine-housekeeper,

that arch-swine whose name is arch-swine
is manipulating the accounts,
with her sickly pale grin at what she's done, unrepentant,
a passable carrot soup if I'm lucky
that beast of a house-witch. If I could be away

      to the forest, *eleison, eleison, eleison,*
sore eyes *adagio molto semplice e cantabile* deaf *benedictus qui venit,*—

Must it be like this, *Factorem cœli et terrae,* must it be?
In the ditch I try to sleep the tramp growls in me atonally,
I growl back my *laudamus te* I neither know
nor attend—I attend! I attend! Attention is what I am! Show

      the boundless storm, *Kyrie eleison*
      for which we were born, *Christe eleison*
      into coarse light, *Kyrie eleison.* I have

inhabited in darkness the miracle of *falter*. On my knees,
I have asked blessing beyond my means I confess reward
more than I could hold.   You know, dear,

> how everything that is despair is despair
> and everything that is not despair is despair. I am, O Sublime

> Fisherman, in the flow exercised
> by the accidentals. How much longer
> to linger here tightly
> let me go, hold me, let me go, hold me, hold me. Everything

that is despair is despair and everything
that is not despair is despair. What
does the Holy Name
for his design
want of me? Perhaps to clip bushes
for the Archbishop. Perhaps to
clean drains. Rest is not possible only to

play repose. I, *Earwig van Breeze-heaving*
play the game of variance. Ah, to clean drains. A beast

> tramples up and down my keyboard—
> I need a Broadwood stretched six yards long:
> more generous incarceration, extended restraint.

> I must have imagined the kiss—but the fluttering of the dress,
> the waving of the dress, the spinning of the dress
> she gave me—but the flouncing of the dress,
> the clouding of the dress, the holiness of the smile,
> the distancing of the dress—Antonie instead of a kiss
> gave me half a crate of *Riesling* left over from the party
> to which I was a not-invited, her *legato* hair tied tight in a sparkling
> headband, while
> > from behind her eyes
> > she measured
> > my irreparable
> > nakedness I swear my naked
> > corpus. I have written

no letters today, have shouted at the maid for spilling soup
on my Shakespeare. She failed to cry, I
put a ladder up to heaven, my routine contention, got shat on,
the usual, the old blessedness.

                              The stairs here got steeper, a man

half-way up was lung-hooting-throat-snapping, I thanked him
out loud for being in more distress than I was,
                    for which forgive me but
could that man contrive a sonata, could he? Could he build
          an *Agnus dei*, could he conjure by stealth
                    a quartet? But
          'That *Beet-heaving,*' they will say,
'he didn't belong in the world, didn't know how to behave' —
          They will say, 'That *Boot-hooven,*
one of the Almighty's mistakes, hardly human at all.' Again

my kitchen maid, I repeat, the kitchen maid, she has a name.
The kitchen maid asked for a day off to visit her sick sister.
I said, 'How sick?' She looked at me. I looked at her. One child

born dead   the next born alive   the next dead   the next
alive   the next dead   the next dead   the next dead between the slats
of winter the glut—I am so tired, so tired. Rising
out of sleep *et incarnatus est* impales me,
                    Heilig, Heilig, Heilig
with every ludicrap breath
                    the whole endeavour,
with every fierce breath rich understanding with vacancy,
with shove-sharp of breath the crucial turn,
with held breath no shagfest, the ache, *Heilig,*
with forgetful breath glory whispering into me,
with every zeal-breath ignorance,
with every h-h-hesitant breath rage,
with joy-breath doubt and debt and shadow,
with lungs sore up the steep shale, *Heilig,*
with torn breath her not opening the door,
with every amity-breath death's grin,
with every, every breath the Unconditional Designer
knows my graft and turns away, *Heilig,* when I

most need Him, with every squirt-squeeze of breath such
waste, loss, defeat, stomach *in tempore belli*,
with every lucky breath
toll-taunt voices at the edge—
                                        I have never wanted
    to cut a man through with a bayonet
    nor to bluster his head off with a howitzer,
    the streets of the city are not for this, we poor bastards all of us,
    with only the thinnest covering of skin. Can a man raid Heaven,

raid Heaven and bring back notes
meant for world-graft-song from the beginning? Forgive me,

        you pig of a maid, my derision,
        forgive me, *Dominus Deus*,
        I have written music for whoever would best pay me,
        forgive me, my soul,
        I have risen up giddy from the affliction of Adam's longing.
        Break me!   Instead of a kiss Antonie

released me with her lace and tippet smile and half a crate
of *Riesling*. If in this fleshy world
she would have
                        leaned into me the way I have seen women do,
what revelation then in my dissonance! What an apprenticeship!
I position myself eyes closed as if she is
                                    leaning into me, a touch
of a lean of a tilt.
                    I am the plaything
of the One Who Gives And Who Takes Away to whom I am
of necessity obedient wholly in debt.
                                    With my house-swine
                                    I attempted my best

maid-politic behaviour and endeavoured to keep her,
hoping she would cook well and not shit-snigger me.
She saw me washing naked almost and she smirked.

    What is *Kyrie* through to *Agnus Dei* worth these days?
    Concert gruel.

The voracious sea I have heard would swallow me:
kind, purposeful.
Wringing the duck's neck the maid said *fuck* three times
by candlelight,
I said it four times *con brio appassionato* dismissing her,
well meant.

Every panicky tributary—
every tributary panicky shambling between tilt-crags
along crack-hollows down between bright shrubs down
by way of fluency-river to the sea-absolute is absolved whole,

but I have been taken sideways towards blocked gullies, into
closed sluice gates, diverted into mud between hawthorn
to be caught, a trapped boar. How

    do I love thee? Let me fumble the ways.
    I love thee with obscure fugal distress,
    with a circumspect *fortissimo* I love thee.
    Eagerly I stagger the byways to run free
    with tenderness—awkward, hoping, broken
    with unease—not with lust only believe this,
    our eyes a bright duet fluent with devotion
    across the Drawing Room, dear, yours
    every spill from the hoard of Heaven's riches,
    yours every note I write in hallowed quiet
    from I do believe the far, fluent reaches.
    Didn't we discover our yes, our yes, defiant?
    In the cool wood imagine coming close.
    Heaven is raining iron bed frames.
                    Every night in the ditch. Yesterday

the Touch Of The Most High did not claim me,
today I was claimed and it was too easy. I am

    a sack of onions shouting *Hosanna* all the parts.
    The nag's tail is my time-keeper my flight exuberant.
    On a clear calm night I offer *Miserere* in advance of payment.
    I am fleshy matter in a sack, I must escape and wake,
    I must burgle my own house, claw back the clues. Grant me

at least one day of uncorrupted pleasure, surely light
wants to catch her here—skin, eyes, hair. If I could be

    a true father, if Karl would—
    I seem to be a grown man—
    Grown men everywhere are fathers.
    Karl needs a fit father, I have the papers
    giving me the right,—If I could have lived

    in a segregate-hut, in a farm cottage,
    in a chapel-adjacent, *pp leggiermente*—
                Every night in the ditch every night

the articulate tramp in the ditch shouts at me I shout back we neither
know nor care who has said what every blessed elation a needle in my
gut he shouts I shout the tramp shouts more loudly I shout back treble
fortissimo where we sleep in the ditch in his skin he tells me what to
do with my *Sanctus* I tell him what to do with his *sempre staccato*
at dawn my genuflection after a good fart brings light. What now

              is required of me?
'It doesn't matter if you live or die.'
But what is required of me?
'See out your time. Snort. Cry.'
But what is being asked of me?
Weeks go by.
'To gorge on meat and honey and wine and on each other.'

    Where elation drives, shame follows,
    rush forward to accept direction
    to the trip-wire,
    repair the fault with stillness
    and risk inertia.

    In Bach no hesitation, in Mozart no wait,
    in both inexhaustible open—in Handel no break until before
    the final *Alleluia*, lovely rain. I say

        heroic to wait
        through the long night

for fresh light
to let fly

from rock into the heavens, poor thing
the child looking for coloured stones innocent
in the river bed, enchanted by

balance, order, unity, decorum, no ecstasy, fear,
interruption as needs be later, later. The fortepiano

must be played at the great trial. Glory *in extremis*
to the Most High Nameable With No Name for
shaggy goats on rocks,
for ragged sheep astray and a mislaid nag in foal,
for the portrait of my beloved
painted already in heaven. I must learn from memory
the squirrel's stretch-leap between branches in the forest,
I must exact flute-breeze through ash,
I must notate the flip-snaps of the horse's tail,
I must weigh the plain kitchen maid's sighs. I am
not patient, days

are rushed past, I hear the capricious angels—
In my prison not these songs a new song. I see

a blind man
on stilts
crossing the river
at night.   Hold me,

let me go, let me go, let me go, hold me. I inhabit
the miracle of *falter*, I neglect the gracious reasoning of the salon,
I make a figure in air until
                    by means of *falter*—
ragged though I am
is the whole work. I work

for them the bastards every morning *Amen* his Utter Highness the
Archduke Archbishop Lord Athletic Toilmaster in the Sanctuary
robed perfumed for Heaven in Fox-Blood Red I am a curse-beggar

with a claim on the raid-wound silence-chastened every pause scars
me daily *Amen* I learn by means of *falter*

on my knees in fame by means of bold *falter*

> to have shambled
> without comfort,
> to have shuffled
> without assurance,
> I must die
> with secret *vivace*.
>
> In the street

a man is playing an accordion made of honey-buzzard feathers,
a clown tip-toeing the pavement is pretending to juggle plums,
a music teacher is shopping for jewels beyond knowledge.
I have pissed in my pot and I have put the pot where it lives
under the bed, I have added in mind a flat to a floating quaver,
I have asked my father wholly to die, to get out of my way.
I have put a ladder up to heaven—got shat on. Now

in chains in shadow here no warmth comes close no sound
  in shadow here no warmth when soul to soul
     in chains in shadow   here submit
  in chains submit be broken now   succumb
              no warmth submit no sound can bring
        that blessed day   submit in chains no warmth
     no warmth comes close no sound can bring that day
                              our soul to soul   in chains
        submit be broken now in chains no warmth
              no hold   no warmth
     in darkness now no   sound   no soul to soul so yield
         to live that day and then   to live
           to live that day our soul to soul when free
       surrender now in chains no warmth submit
              submit be broken   now   surrender, yield
     abandon thought of warmth of sound   of when—

if I could fall out of bed,—
if I could contrive a fall,

if I could crawl to the table, put the pen to work. Yield

    to shadow now no warmth, abandon thought,
    be broken now submit O soul succumb,
    no warmth comes close no soul to soul no hold,
    in darkness then submit to faith, be found.
    A yell for voices shouting every bar shouting
                until
who am I to put my name to the Divine work? Confess rather
my work's defects, what might have been claimed had I been
the proper strait for it. I plead

    intestinal grief my
    ugly infertile imploding innards
    where leeches have sucked me barren,
I plead
    I have been solitary to get the work done,
I plead
    I have struggled through without affection,
    without bodily comfort,
    mocked every day, every day
    by puppets who think they know better. Holy Maker
    why have you done this to me? Forgive me,
                     it must be,
                     I am your servant,
    every long day to
    speak out of turn to find and lay bare, the making
      wholly yours, but—this one *but*—
            I have sweated
            in pain my own
               desire
             for holiness
            with intent
            on fire-wings
         discovered
          echo
             from my heart—
Forgive me,
    in your mercy explain. *Explain!*

One day
      we will be united
        all
      in love. Nearly

done now, *van Bait-hanging's* blood-lurch
in a world worn through with noisy rutting,
to leave behind the corpse of a dog that
  scuffing for scraps
    had a voice once. **"**

Towards the line

—two—

And following them

And following them without instruments the musicians,
and following them without microphones the commentators,
and following them in this bright light the sleepwalkers,
and following them brushless on his knees the old painter,
and following him painted red like a nose an Abrams M1A2 tank,
   the crew in wizards' hats, their eyes shining, their ears dead,
and following the tank the Generals in their frocks with medals,
   slipping and sliding, two of them in tears, waving their hankies,
and here come the embroidered banners as if carried by no one and
   caught by the sea breeze, shat on by gulls, out from the museum,
and after them the lone Minister, with briefcase and sandwiches,
and following the Minister a cartload of cyanide for the fish,
and following a little way behind a woman who is thinking.

She is thinking of newspapers thrown overboard from a ferry,
she is thinking of all that news getting washed out of the paper,
she thinks of the ink darkening the waves in patterns,
the black blood floating free through the opinion columns
smirking this not that in the world where consciousness
has yet to be understood, O my Giddy Aunt the Renaissance!
She thinks of the paper folded and refolded by blue-grey waves,
opened up and turned, opened up and turned again, opened up
and folded, opened up again, bundled soggy now, disintegrating,
word-flesh leaving the body towards its utmost reclusiveness,
the big news and the small news all washed out together,
the ink that made the one mixing with the ink that made the other,
she is thinking the paper bare of all its words now, bare of them all.

And following the woman who is thinking come the sellers of souvenirs,
and following the sellers of souvenirs the actors dressed as monks,
and following the actors dressed as monks the thin trumpeters,
and after them the nurses pushing the beds of the living wishing to die,
and after the nurses pushing the living wishing to die come the postmen
   casting letters into the crowd for anyone to catch,
and following the postmen the baby trying to walk like a soldier,
and after the baby trying to walk like a soldier the glass-blowers,
and after the glass-blowers the road itself curling.

We came then

We came then to the extreme garden,
I took off my hat and you did,
or you took off yours and I did,
you took off your shoes, I took off mine,
we didn't look at each other as we went in
and then we did, you said, *Write this*,
or I said it. We spread our towels on the grass,
sat facing the inner garden
and looked at each other for the first time again.
                                        Rain came,
we sat and got wet, the flowers shone,
water dripped down our eyes, I said, *Do write this*,
or you said it. The paths made holy patterns,
you sneezed or I did,
there was a toothbrush in the dog daisies,
I pointed to the ferns, or you did,
we walked until we became giddy
with eyes. I would have brought you a chair,
you would have brought one for me,
we said together, *It will rain for ever*,
or we said it together, or we said it together,
you touched my hand
with your finger, we kept walking, we paused a lot,
there was no horizon,
I said, *What next?*, quietly, or you did.

Book

In July 1987 I bought from Alan Halsey
at his shop in Hay-on-Wye
a book he'd bought as one of a quantity
from Roy Fisher, whose name is in it, Robert Duncan's

'The truth and life of myth', published 1968
(the year of my ordination and the barricades in Paris)
by the Sumac Press, Michigan,
and I took it back to Birmingham.

I read it then, or some of it, honestly some of it,
and while I recall nothing of what it said I remember
it mattered to me, was big with fertile ideas.

I recall speculating as to why Roy had
disposed of/ let go of/ had had enough of/
parted from it.

And looking at it again now
away for two weeks in Falmouth: Roy had
marked this passage:

'But what I speak of here in the terms of a theology
is a poetics. Back of each poet's concept of the poem
is his concept of the meaning of form itself; and his
concept of form in turn where it is serious at all
arises from his concept of the nature of the universe,
its lifetime of form, or even, for some, its lifelessness
or formlessness.'

That last section Roy had underlined.
The only other marked passage (Roy's again)
says this:

'In the belief in the Hidden Zaddik, the divine
wisdom that the least of men may be illumined by,
the Chassidic masters speak not only to the Jewish
community, but to our common humanity.'

The book cost me £4.50.
I don't know what Roy was paid for it,
most likely he sold Alan a job lot.

Through the window where I am writing this
there's a rather bedraggled looking sycamore,
big bunches of seeds still hanging off it
and some of the leaves turning already, we're in
September now, just,
and across to my right, just visible,
small boats in the bay and up the Penrhyn river
and at the far side of them, above Flushing,
bright green fields.

Borrow these?

If you want to borrow *bridge* and *flow*,
if you want to borrow *mud* and *deep* and *yes*
and *waterfall* and *pool* and *coracle* and *tunny*,
if you want to borrow these and
see where they take you—oh imagine—or if you want to
borrow *kindling* and *old newspapers*
and *sunlick* and through a *magnifying glass*
start a *frilly fire* to keep someone far away
warm or *rusing* for some quite other—
oh you know—purpose, perhaps *heart*-shook,
and while we're about it
borrow *skim* as well and *skin, stock,*
borrow *wistful* and *roll* and *line.*
Not mine, of course, to lend, any of these,
this is a *dance* only of the *to* and *fro,*
of the *ask* and *yes*, of the *ask* and *no.*
Do what you will

with *life, love* and *death,*

and you could borrow *trip* and *flinging*
and what might you do with *slip, bone, bake*
and *brain* and *ha-ha* and *well now*, and *turning*
and the awesome *if, when* and *so,*
and I suggest *ship*, please do borrow also
lease and *whim, glow, sad* and *O.*

They could be thrown out, these words, or quick,
sigh forth, borrow, chew, click, peel,
ventilate and brim them.

The gully hermits
For Tess Biddington

Something should be said now in respect of the gully hermits,
for the record,
that they are, to find the words, Christ with deep-grasped eyes,
for remembering,
tired as a shelf, where the shaggy cliff seems to overhang easy,
to note it,
up and down, boots soaked through, a nod, shifty, a finger,
to give it shape,
preferment without title except fluke, bristleworm, thrip, whip,
in shadow,
hand in no hand but in the rush of air, in nettle, in bramble,
to keep this on file,
how the rocks lock almost, how sanctuary, to seek the words,
to map it,
where secret brides, to find the words, to translate longing,
document it,
the face in the rock when otherly lit, *I swear*, lichen-tasting,
keep a record.
the flower called candle, Christ in the ditch-turn disintegrating,
keep a record,
Hello, remember that *Hello,* its echo *Hello, Hello* for nights after,
keep a record,
nothing comfortable here, to shake the words, no ship, boat,
keep a record,
not even a coracle, a plank, branch, even a toy mock-cutter,
keep a record,
a mark on a stone, blood on a leaf to be interpreted, day's night,
keep a record,
the bargain, the deal, the instrument of promise, the up-down-up,
keep a record,
no camera steady, only to imagine if the light is right, emerald—
keep a record—
aquamarine, pitchblende, malachite, lung-strike, gannet, gull,
keep a record,
prints in mud, overprints, whisper bouncing off rock, tug-flight,
hold it.

I think every day

I think every day I must swim in my blood,
I must swim in my blood to find out who I am,
I must travel where my blood takes me
to places I have not visited before,
to the far reaches to find out who I am,
to the precision of myself if I can discover where that is,
in my blood's knowledge lose and find myself,
travel by being taken, swim without swimming,
every day I think I must do it,
every day thought intends it.

A dog with three legs dances to a blind flute player,
the flute player turns to where he knows the sun used to be
at this time of day, the dog does a high turn and lands flat.
This cannot be named, says a passer-by, cannot, cannot.

I think every day I must set out into my blood,
I must rush through my blood to find out who I am,
I must journey where my blood leads
to places for which I have no names,
to the far reaches of my blood to find out who I am,
to the core of myself if I can discover where that is,
for drinking, shaping, into shadows and netted light,
or to somewhere quite other, to my Forbidden City
to find out what is forbidden in me.

He ran for them

He ran for them, ran for them, ran and ran
in the uplands of urban, urban.
He was awarded gleam-gifts from friends and the friends of friends
who would pay in kind, and smile and pay more for his blisters
and more for his backache
and more for his having slipped and broken an ankle almost,

because this was intimate between them,
it was secret running, he ran for them alone, ran and ran for them,
he represented them in the uplands, uplands,
leaving them behind where they were in urban, urban, waiting
for when he would return and smile
and show his blisters
and his backache
and the ankle which he had broken almost,
and they would put into his hands twice the gifts they'd pledged
in the ache of their own hearts,
this was what he did for them, this was the work he did,
this was his vocation,

then further into the uplands, uplands, further,
so that his chest hurt,
so that his neck could barely support his head,
so that along a sharp edge he fell almost
and along the next ridge he did fall, went toppling over into shale,
was scarred as he rolled and slid down, down,
and was collected,

and their eyes said, you have been to the uplands, uplands for us,
you have run yourself into pain, near to death even,
we owe you more than we have,
we owe you more than urban, urban can give,

and the next day he was off again into the uplands, uplands,
running, running,
running for his friends and for the friends of friends,
doing it for them, for them,
beyond their means.

She photographs the ruins

Day by day she photographs the wild ruins for them,
first thing out of bed she is there among the walls.
Through the heat of the day she has her eye on them,
and in the evening she is there in slant light.

Each pillar and arch she photographs day by day
and again the next day from a worm's eye angle.
She is in place on time as the seasonal light changes,
in air thick with dust from siege-fires the ruins

must be recorded, her brief requires it, with zest.
She has caught today the ghost with the broken arm.
Nothing she can do about the pain, she says, turning
to the font where she misses by a millisecond

the baptism into the community of a shag-headed man
released from the despair of travel into commonality.
She will watch with her other eye for a spectral re-run
as she works her body's sight over the tiles and ribs.

She catches now in a storm the remains of the belfry,
here come the full flesh of geese, lightning on their backs,
making for the monk-made lake where fish prepare
for her camera little moans of leap, flash and turn.

They want more, the people who at night are paying her,
prayer must show in the prints, they say, and song,
there must be urgency of confession and remission of sin,
the photos so far, they say, aching, are too thin, too thin.

The weeds know something

The weeds in my garden need rain and plenty of it,
the trip to Catatonia is off, I'll stay in my own bed,
I've read the *Story of O*, it will have to do, and now

that I have Ginsberg on CD and Groucho Marx on
DVD and the forecast is showers in the morning
I shall stop ageing and after breakfast apply myself.

I'm thinking to crush some kidney beans and pods
of dementia and blueberries and wrinkles from Dolgelly
for colours, to paint my way out of deep shadow,

and when the steam train at the steep incline falters
I'll be waiting with my brush, young again, to be
described on local radio between songs as a vagrant.

Mary who you don't know, not that Mary, another,
worked in a vineyard once, she and her friend Jane,
they got tied in knots over their wages in French,

so stole a goat, ran away with it one night to Spain,
to Granada to show the goat the Alhambra, they said.
Singing to myself I met Mary in a gale of prayer-meal.

I shall stop ageing now and after breakfast apply myself,
to the weeds in my garden needing rain and plenty of it,
here's *Kaddish* in that holy, sweet voice, gone from us,

and at the same time the puns on DVD, while Mary,
in the living room feeding the goat porridge and crisps
of eclamentia phones Jane where she's stoned in Bath.

The manuscripts
For Victoria Field

One manuscript says he saw the way farsightedly,
while the other says he was delivered blindfold,

one manuscript says she came down the wild hillside,
while another says she arrived in the dark by boat.

One manuscript says he was crippled from falling,
while another says he was as fit as a hare and running,

one manuscript says she was dressed in goat skin,
while another says she was wearing blooded wool.

One manuscript says the poem was blown right away
by the storm that came up over the stepping stones,

while another says it was never put into writing,
only carried in the heart until all who knew it died.

One manuscript says she was singing *The lost ewe*,
another says she was humming a wordless tune,

and there are so many variants about what this was
in fragments of bleached skin or blatant forgeries:

*Gone is the bright track, / Slipping the harness, /
Dream thy journey, my love, / The saddle-bag, away then,*

and for centuries poets have attempted the reconstruction:
where the sightless met the singer, where the lame the goat,

where their running echoed around the world as thunder,
where the storm subsided and the day was bright and clear,

how the road over the mountains was in the sky almost,
how their ways became melded flesh into one body,

where these two resolved or dissolved their passion,
where words were perfected or failed utterly.

Despair

Reading the poetry of James K. Baxter

I need you, fellow poets,
scramblers after the right words,
turning up, bringing a packed lunch.

The right words for what?
I need another cup of tea,
another walk.

In the rollcall for the gift of despair
silence is speech.
Out of it, the memory,
the poem.

Little boy who runs along beside me,
wide-eyed, in tears almost, chuckling,
skipping and hopping, his little heart crowding,
a sigh escaping him almost
huger than the big bang.

Come along, come along.

Queuing with Trakl

In response to the poetry of Georg Trakl

While I'm waiting I can admire the daffodils,
while I'm waiting I can listen to the birds panting,
while I'm waiting I can smell the perfumes of herbs,
while I'm waiting I can be glad of a damp brick shed
falling in on itself, while I'm waiting
I can talk with the donkeys who think they are horses
who think they are camels who think they can fly,
while I'm waiting I can hold on to what I haven't got.

> *He applied to join a lonely hearts club*
> *but they replied they weren't that lonely.*

While I'm waiting I can enjoy the hills in the distance,
while I'm waiting I can play at rearranging words.

> *Did you know about the man who shot an arrow*
> *into the air — and missed?*

While I'm waiting I can pick up the tune coming
down the line, while I'm waiting I can do a bit of
landscape gardening, while I'm waiting I can
clean the windows and polish the floor and
put the kettle on.

> *Nobody knows a poet is alive until they're dead.*

While I'm waiting I can deny the slaughterhouse,
while I'm waiting I can enjoy the terrible privilege
of despair, so that when Spring says one thing—

> *I told my psychiatrist I had suicidal tendencies*
> *and he said, 'From now on you can pay in advance.'*

While I'm waiting I can deny the reality of the queue,
while I'm waiting I can pick my nose.

> *What do you say when you meet God and he sneezes?*

While I'm waiting I can pretend the queue is for me alone,
while I'm waiting I can notice the forget-me-nots,
while I'm waiting I can crowd closer to those ahead of me and
to those following, while I'm waiting I can smile for cameras,
while I'm waiting I can sunbathe in black-blue light.

Here's Gary Snyder on film
For Glenn Storhaug

Here's Gary Snyder on film
with Ginsberg—dead—
and a picture of Kerouac—dead—

and on television yesterday evening
the 1965 Albert Hall poetry explosion,
including Ginsberg—dead.

I am watching the clouds
through the window
in the mirror.

Here's Snyder now on tape to a live audience
re-rehearsing his poems.

The clouds are faster now and thinner,
there's more blue,
through the window
in the mirror.

Snyder in print is on the table,
he has set down plenty of it,
what he knows. And alive still.

The clouds are passing through such clear blue
through the window
in the mirror and outside

in the arboretum I am trying to
sing a descant by myself
trying to get up
above it all
          into that thrilling,
flying, straining, smiling, hurting
O beautiful, throat-full high notes,
I want to be up there
higher and higher
and to break
and to cry and cry and cry.

Inviting the dead

It is not easy to persuade the dead
to come and read their poems,
they seem otherwise engaged.

It is not exactly that they are unwilling,
they can hear distant applause
and for a moment they like it,
then they forget.

They need a bit of persuading, the dead,
they need keeping to the task,
they are apt to say yes
then not turn up. I have found myself
with an empty platform and a room full
of expectant and accusing eyes.
They promised, I say,
and I am booed off the stage.

How tasty the coffee and biscuits,
surely these will attract the dead,
they can smell the bouquet surely
and they need the sugar to psych them up a bit
for the reading. And I have ready,
typed up, their record of achievement
and a few special words I have rehearsed.
Their accomplishments and my welcome
will roll off my tongue.

But no, they do not come. The dead,
I mutter to myself
on the way home after locking up,
are whimsical buggers, I can't depend on them.
But I will ask again, I know I will,
I will programme them in,
sell tickets, wait for those soft footsteps,
those cherished voices.

She's gone to Minehead

She's gone to Minehead,
she wanted to take the house with her,
she couldn't face leaving it,
she couldn't face leaving that room,
she couldn't face leaving that mirror,
she couldn't face being out of that dress.

She kept the dress on all night
and the next morning early
before it was light
she crept out
and went to Minehead.
Why Minehead she didn't say,
it was her secret,
and we left it at that.

Bo-bo

Bo-bo wasn't on his way home but
with absurd stealth was
advancing towards the mausoleum
of the illegitimate.

It takes a while (I know) for the great tent
to come clean—dirty fucking place—
the moon even is reluctant
to connive in allowing definition.

The dog that attends at the gate (I know)
will bite if a blue-grey bell
rings in its head. Male or female (I don't know)
it keeps its bark to itself,
the way a coffin rarely opens,
even at this time of night.

Bo-bo (I suspect) is thinking, home would be nice,
while his bread knife is out ready to kill the dog
after an avowal of friendship.

In blue-grey light the mausoleum
has what the guide books invariably describe
as demonic glory. Some people (not me) claim
to have experienced it,
to have seen it glow 'like a turtle on heat'.

Bo-bo cannot use the knife (I am not surprised),
so the dog leaps at him, at his neck,
not to kill
but to leave him there bloody and
sick with failure,
to be found by a tourist with a guide book
open and wet.

The ward now
coming in to land

Poems and transcriptions
from a residency with
South Birmingham Mental Health NHS Trust

WE MIGHT SAY we find words when we need them, we might say words find us, we might say words are essentially shared and we help each other find what we need. There is the therapeutic argument while also there is the statistic that competing for highest suicide and addiction rates have been professional writers of poetry and fiction. There may be a view, too, that poetry is good for floating with on a summer's afternoon in the sun.

If I try to locate my own writing, I want to say it is a response to the 'Other'. This is not distinctly a religious 'Other', nor is it necessarily personal; clearly it is not something in a void—writing implies connecting somehow. Perhaps it is related to the notion of (experience of) vocation. Perhaps it relates to the strangeness of finding ourselves here on this planet to which we have, as coherently as we can, to respond. I forget the 'Other', I read my notes and remind myself, I make poems. If I'm asked again, or if I ask myself, the 'Other' makes a reappearance. Or, rather, it is a name for what I don't understand that compels.

I am remembering an elderly woman, in a room by herself, in 'Continuing Care'. As a shorthand I shall say she was a case of dementia. She talked on and on without pause. I sat and began to transcribe what she was saying. This is a part of it:

> 'She didn't know what to do so she left it,
> she never bothered about it so that's all she knew,
> she used to say, write for a fifteen,
> we used to say give her fifteen and that way all we knew,
> fifteen it was all right and they knew,
> we used to pull this end, that's all,
> that's all we knew, she didn't know so she talked,
> so she just denied it, that's all I knew,
> so she said I didn't know no more
> I never knew no more, I didn't, I didn't,
> so you didn't have it at home
> that was all right then,
> he knew what it was, no harm in it,
> he never knew nothing about it,
> no knowing, no nothing because he knew nothing,
> we were nothing against it,
> lovely, thank you very much goodnight ta-ta,
> I didn't know, we have to wait till whatsit comes down,
> we used to say that's all we used to pray for,
> he said he didn't know what it was,—'

What struck me was how musical this was, what rhythm it has. And although I don't know the meaning of what is being said, clearly there is meaning. Something is being repeated over and over, it is in some way being remembered and self-related. I am in no position medically to do more than wonder whether this could be worked with.

And here is the first of the ethical questions. So far as I could tell, this woman was not even aware of my presence. No conversation was possible, I couldn't show her what I had transcribed, nor ask her permission to relate it on. My reasoning is that to have her words heard may possibly be of interest in a way that may help other people—and throw light also on the shaping of language.

Our everyday speech has meaning, sometimes trivial, sometimes urgent and profound, sometimes confused, but when we say someone is 'talking to herself', 'to himself', what is this? Surely we 'talk to ourselves' all the time, sometimes aloud, mostly silently. So what is the borderline between different kinds of speech-meaning, between different kinds of self-experiencing and of communicating? This is another transcription, from an elderly woman:

> 'Mum, can I go?!
> Mum, Mum! Oh dear our Mum's packing up.
> Mum! Can I go?!
> I want my Mum.
> Dad, dad! I don't know what's the matter with him,
> I want, where is it?
> Mum, I want to die, I want to die,
> Mum, I want to die, I do, I do!
> Mum, I want to die,
> Mum, Mum. Mum!
> Mum, I want to go!
> Mum, I'm dying to go!
> Mum, Mum, Mum!
> She didn't dare tell me, did she?
> I don't know what to do, I don't know what to do!
> Mum, Mum, I want to go, quick!
> Mum, Mum, Dad!
> Please, Mum, I want to go, I want to go.
> I'm dying to go, Mum!
> Dad, could I have a drink, Dad?
> Dad, can I go?!

Dad, Mum!
Mum, where's me handbag?
Mum, tell me, tell me!'

And this following: one woman, who was usually with another woman who said very little. So there was a kind of 'talking to', but with a
relentless momentum:

'She's got some tea, has she? No, she's got no tea at all. Have you got
any tea? I'm dying for a cup of tea, my mouth's really dry . . . What are
they playing at this morning? They don't know, they don't know, they
don't know what they're doing. Waiting now for each other. Yes, she's
gotta wait now, she's waiting now, where she went I don't know, I don't
know, terrible, terrible! She's got to wait now, she's got to wait now,
but you can't find her. Well, I've been waiting for ages and I've got
nobody . . . You try that, you try that, try one of them . . . That's why
she had to get a new pair of socks, she should have socks. What am I
going to do now? I'm going to the police station. They're new socks,
brand new socks. They're supposed to be new socks. Where are they?
I don't know. Have you got my socks there, please? Not them? Lost
them? Don't be daft, they're new socks. They must have gone abroad.
Where's all the damned socks going to?, that's what I want to know.
Nurse, where are all my socks going? What did I have? I haven't had a
pair of socks yet. I'm going down the police station. Nurse, have you
got anything for me?'
    Rediscovering these writings for myself these few years later, I have
to do a double-take to remember that the following is a poem of my
own, arising from sitting for hours in those wards, assuming a voice:

Who's that? Have I seen her before?
Will she get me out of here?
That person with the—what's it called?—the *board*—
and the pen dangling off it. Clip-clop. Clap-trap. Clip-frame.
Ah, here's that woman who smiled at me,
    will she smile at me again today? She's smiling at that old—
What's he want with her? His jumper smells.
A lovely smile, though, lovely.

I don't like that one, she brought me weak squash.
Is this today or is it still yesterday?

Is it perhaps tomorrow already?
Is this the tea coming or just an empty trolley?

Do I have anyone left to visit me?
What happened to Charlie? Did he die?
Why? Didn't he love me? He loved me once, said he did.

Who's that telling a joke to the woman with the nice smile?
Is he a doctor?
Looks like he's telling a joke. Say it louder!
Will he get me out of here?

If I ask for a cup of tea, will I be a nuisance?
Will they think I'm a nuisance?
Speaking out of turn. I spoke out of turn once, . . . When was that?

Who's that in those flowery trousers? Do I know her?
Is she a doctor? Why is she talking to that man who's
always half asleep and not to me? I'm awake. I think I am.
When's the tea coming?
I wonder what kind of biscuits they'll give us today.
Did Charlie die? He's not here, I don't think he's here.
He didn't say he was going to die.
Did he?
Did I miss it?

I watched a woman and a man, not related, walk and walk and walk
about the rooms, she usually with her arm in his. It was rare for either
of them to speak and when they did it was a word or two. I *imagined*
what she was saying in herself:

If I hold your arm
I'll know who I am,
if I follow you around
holding your arm
and if we sit together on the sofa
I'll know who I am
and why I am. Where you go
I'll go, holding your arm,
where you sit I'll sit,
I'll know who I am then
and why I am.

And again and again in these wards, time seemed to mean something
different. I wrote the following as it happened, very, very slowly:

> A man half bent over on the sofa,
> eyes down, asleep or awake.
> As assistant puts a mug of tea in his hand
> but he can't hold it or isn't ready,
> she puts it on the sideboard next to him.
>
> With the cup shakily in his hand now
> he raises it slowly to his . . . But where to go?
> The cup goes to his glasses, almost touches them,
> then slowly down again,
> then up again, this time half way to his mouth.
>
> The cup is on the sideboard again.
> A biscuit has been put in his hand.
> Using both hands shaking and with tiny movements
> he tries to break the biscuit.
> With a small piece of it he tries to find his mouth.
> He fails and lowers his hand again very slowly.
> His left hand holds the biscuit half away.
> His right hand has gone right down past his knees.
> It comes up again.
> He achieves breaking the biscuit again
> and with his right hand reaches his mouth
> with a tiny piece
> and gets it in.
>
> He has found the cup of tea on the sideboard
> and holding it in his right hand
> he is drinking from it very slowly,
> all the while his head down.
>
> He seems to have finished the tea
> and is trying to reach the floor with the cup
> to put it there. Working it into place,
> not quite reaching, . . .
> now he has done it.
>
> Now very slowly he reaches down
> and picks it up again, a short distance, by its rim.

Now he is putting it down again.

The cup isn't empty.
The assistant picks it up, saying,
'Do you want to finish your tea?'
and puts the cup in his hands.
He cups his hands around the cup
and she helps it to his lips.
He drinks a little and lowers it again
and she takes it away.

He has most of the custard cream left
and after trying to break off a piece, his hands shaking,
puts it on the sofa beside him.

He tries to stand
and very slowly turns and is soon
heaped about the end of the sofa,
his weight greater than his power to shift it.
Two assistants help him up
and sit him back on the sofa.
One says, 'Stay there.'
But he wants to move, so they
help him up and he walks or is walked
across the room and into an armchair.
One of the assistants pulls out the footrest
which tips the chair back.
She puts the stool under the footrest to support it.
She adjusts the head rest, pats his chest,
and says, 'There, have a rest.'
He closes his eyes and is still.

I suppose we humans, like any other animal, rail at confinement,
it's not natural to us. Hence this imagined voice, of a woman who was
for real on the move the whole time:

The thing to do here is to keep moving,
keep moving, keep moving, keep moving,
from this chair to the low round table,
sit on the table, rest a moment,
keep walking, into the corridor,
I must be intent, I must keep walking

forwards as accurately as I can,
keep moving along the corridor,
now turn around and keep moving,
miss the door, get through the space,
sit on the round table, keep my face furrowed
with intent, keep moving,
get up, keep moving, sideways if necessary,
sit on the arm of the chair, then keep moving,
the point here is to keep moving,
first as far as the round table,
sit on it a moment, up again, forwards
if I can keep going forwards, keep moving,
get through the door hole
into the corridor, in the corridor now,
sideways as sideways seems to be necessary,
turn around, back along the corridor,
through the door hole,
reach the round table, sit on it
a moment, move on, sit on the arm
of the chair, move on to the rectangular table,
sit there a moment, keep moving,
keep moving with intent, keep moving, —

In the dementia-assessment day ward I sat with a small group of people and engaged easily in conversation, and I asked questions. I was able later to put what they each had said into poem form, to type it up and give it to them. This is everyday coherent life-telling. This was Charles's poem.

Oh yes, we had a cine camera,
we filmed anything that was going,
family events, the kiddies playing
in the pool in the garden,
playing with sand, making mud pies
and stuff like that, getting filthy dirty,
bless 'em. Thirty years ago now.

I used to love photography years ago,
the worst thing then was putting the film in,
a lovely film then half of it's black,
I've done that a few times.

The trouble is they're so easy to do now,
just press the switch. Hit and miss, it was.

I've a picture of the Home Guard—
my Dad was a sergeant.
I lost some friends, they didn't deserve it,
they didn't deserve it,
lots of them didn't come back,
friends of mine.

My grandson has just become a barrister.
The progression of photographs,
it's absolutely beautiful,
one shot, one photo,
and you'll never get it again.

I believe this way of working can catch someone's voice and turn of phrase, selecting but not otherwise editorialising. This is not my poem. When he spoke of his friends—young men—killed in the war, Charles began to cry. This isn't stated in the poem but perhaps the poem suggests it, his words carry that strong feeling.

One day, in one of the Continuing Care centres in the suburbs, I looked out through a window, knowing I was the next day to travel by air to Edinburgh, to give a poetry reading. I suppose hospital staff occasionally—perhaps often—have these crunch moments. I wrote this:

Whose is that sky out there?
Whose are those clouds?
Whose are those golden leaves
as they get caught by the wind,
as they fall, whose are they?
Whose is that sunshine out there,
whose is that brightness?
Whose is that sky out there,
whose are those clouds?
Whose is that rain out there,
whose is that rainbow?
Whose are those falling leaves,
whose is that sky?

It's a 'who owns the world?' question and it is too easy—as with so much of what I found myself feeling and writing and saying—to jump to easy conclusions. I have wondered, though, in relation to dementia and to mental disorders generally, how differently might we be living as a 'culture', as a collective of thinking and feeling people? Are certain kinds of lives—more full of activity, strong relationship and creative awareness?—less likely to fall prey to illness? I have wondered about what is perhaps the narrowness of the overall (educational, cultural, political) sense of who and how we are.

For the AGM while I was there, in the year 2000, I was asked to read some poems, and this one following I wrote for the occasion:

This generation

This generation will take to its grave
the songs that got it through wars:
We'll hang out the washing on the Siegfried Line,—
Let's all go down the Strand,—
Knees up, Mother Brown,—

this generation will take to its grave
the songs it knew from generations past:
There is a tavern in the town,—
In Dublin's fair city, where the girls are so pretty,—
Drink to me only with thine eyes,—
Good night, ladies,—

this generation will take to its grave
its enlistment numbers:
$$76249071$$
      rattled off,
$$29061409$$

and it will take to its grave poems:
The curfew tolls,—
The boy stood on the burning deck,—
Earth has not anything to show more fair,—
What passing bells for these who die as cattle?—
        'Daffodils,' she says, waking up in the corner,

and this generation has in its memory
and in its memory of memories, the workhouse,

the madhouse, trams, pretty ankles, Brylcream,
the mangle, the farthing, corned beef, Bovril, spam,
the wireless, Tommy Handley, the Beverley Sisters,
the back row at the cinema, *Abide with me*,
O come all ye Faithful, Our Father,

and when 'Dust to dust, ashes to ashes'
is said at the grave of this generation
something will have died that it carried
in its head, all lovely,
and wounded.

In the adult acute wards the questions, while overlapping, seem different, not least because the expectation is that a patient—a *service-user*—will be out of there sooner or later to continue their life with as much wellbeing as possible. Conversation is part of the life of the ward, although some people are 'in a world of their own'.

This next poem is wholly my own, but it began from my seeing a young woman where the poem says she was, in the hospital yard. She said nothing and I don't think she saw me—I was some distance away. I don't recall now if I told someone she was there—I like to think I did but I don't remember. In the poem I am presuming to speak in her voice and I have been taken to task for this (while most often—at public readings—there have been no objections). And if I had simply presented this poem as coming from my empathetic imagination, I assume I would have been accepted as a fiction-maker, someone whose task it is to wonder aloud.

Nevertheless, the question remains: my right to her voice. Looked at more affirmatively, the question might be whether the poem can in any way illuminate her situation beyond or in addition to what would be noted and communicated by a psychiatrist or other healthcare professional, or indeed by way of whatever words she could speak of her own.

If I sit out here with the rubbish in the rain,
if I sit here not far away but outside
with the stuff chucked out in the rain,

if what might tenuously be described as me
is outside the walls of the constructed in-place
in the rain with the discarded bits and pieces,

if I can get really wet and alone and known
as total rubbish, if the lorry will come quickly
and take me without even noticing there's a human

so-called to the tip, if no explanation is given
because none is needed and I'm taken away with the
chairs broken on their sides, with the filing cabinet—

if someone who might be expected to know
is asked where I've gone, how beautifully
alarmed the faces, not caring and caring
who I was and where I've gone, wet

into the back of the lorry cracked and crunched
and away to the tip with the broken sunshade,
with the broken glass, with the toys,

all gone, all gone, all surplus to requirements,
all cracked, crunched, tipped and me with them.

Because I was for a couple of days a week in the hospital or in its outlying centres, I became more aware of what I was encountering elsewhere, not least at bus stops. The following is my poem, but was written only because at a bus stop a woman was talking, swearing and, if it was addressed to someone, that person was not present. The poem supposes reflection later:

I had to get my bad words out,
it's not something I would normally do
you understand but it was one of those occasions
when nothing else would do. You understand?

The really bad ones,
the ones I keep in reserve for such a moment,
there was nothing for it but to get them out
and bloody-well use them
if you'll excuse my Martian.

You might think you've heard bad
but you haven't heard bad till you've heard
my bad, believe me, and I got them out, I had to.

If I hadn't have got the words out,
if I hadn't have got those words out right then,
the bad ones, the really bad ones,
God knows what would been the state of my insides.

You don't ever want to be around me, my friend,
when the bad words have to be brought out.
If you ever see that look on face, my dear friend,
keep your bloody distance,
stay out of earshot,
I won't have lost the plot,
I'll just be getting the bad words out
like any reasonable person,
like the person I am.

And at another stop, it was not difficult to transcribe what a very irate man was saying, over and over, waiting for a number 50:

There aren't any 50s,
there aren't any 50s, fuck it,
it's no use waiting in Bradford Street,
there aren't any 50s,
fuck it, there aren't any 50s,
it's no use waiting in Bradford Street,
there aren't any 50s,
there aren't any 50s, so fuck it,
Social Security, fuck 'em,
there aren't any 50s,
so fuck it.

So I became interested in the borderlands of language, of experience, of consciousness in all of us. I sat for many hours of half days in one of the adult acute wards. I had conversations when I could, I wrote poems and when this was possible gave copies to the relevant person. My poems were pinned to the notice board, I did a reading to a users' event in the canteen, the poems were presented at some staff meetings and at a local conference. Subsequently I have included some in public readings.

In the ward, a woman with whom no real to and fro of conversation seemed possible, said—and repeatedly said—the following. Not that this 'poem' was repeated again and again, but not far off it, perhaps in a different order. The poem is an amalgam-transcription. I did respond to her at the time but was not able to shift us to anything else:

> This is my ship,
> every book in the library here is about me,
> but we're not going anywhere
> because the ship is made of brick.
>
> I won't set the fire alarm off with my cigarette
> because this is a ship
> and the ship is our own, isn't it?
> Safety-first, isn't it?
>
> Everyone in here I have to guess,
> but they are to do with me,
> over there are real plants,
> over there are real flowers,
> the sea is everywhere,
> it's underneath us,
> I happen to have more money than the Queen.
>
> Nothing really happens on the ship,
> if there was a lot of sea
> we'd float, wouldn't we?

What seems to me so striking about this is the strength of the metaphor. Here we were in a rather dull room and in her imagination it was a ship. If there was sea around and under us, we could sail away. Metaphor-making is a crucial aspect of poetry-making and I wondered if this couldn't be worked with towards her recovery.

It is uncanny—or obvious, really—how speech becomes poem. The following needed very little making, beyond hearing it:

> I've been so bloody tired
> for a bloody long time,
> tea's bloody cold,
> it's always the same.
>
> I come in here thirsty
> and this is what I get,
> a teapot full of bloody
> tea that's certainly wet

but not hot, I'm seeing red,
I want hot bloody tea,
I've been so bloody tired,
it's bloody being me.

And a phrase, a thought, a way of being, can take on form:

Let me have a cup of tea
and a cigarette
and I'll write the poem,

here's the tea trolley now
and I've got a cigarette,
then I'll write the poem.

Time out with a cup of tea
and a nice long cigarette
and I'll write the poem.

The poem will come out right
after a cup of tea
and a cigarette,

just listen to this poem sing
when I've had my tea
and time in the smoke room,

a cup of tea
and a cigarette
then this'll be the poem, just wait.

For a group I was working with at an out-patient centre, I wrote a poem to illustrate metaphor. Beginning as a mere exercise on my part, I found the image was coming from deep inside me: this was not a mock-up, it was (as I said to the group) my poem:

Can you see me swimming through the deep ocean
trying to reach you on the island?
Can you see me kicking against the big waves
trying to reach the safety of land?
I'm sure if you see me you will come out in the boat
and find me clawing my way through the water,

you will raise the alarm and help will arrive
as we come into land, the log fire will be lit,
the table will be spread with good things,
and I'll be in the arms of those who love me.
If I can make myself hear through the roar
of the ocean, if I can fight my way through the waves,
or just let go and let the sea take me.

And from conversations, from listening to what people sitting in
the acute ward were saying, metaphors showed themselves:

Inside the concrete bunker
there is a glasshouse,
in the glasshouse
we walk through treacle

and back through it
and sideways through it
and we fly through it
and crawl in it
and we hop, skip and jump in it

until the tea trolley comes
and we have a tea trolley party,
a cup of tea in the treacle party,

and then we walk through treacle again
inside the glasshouse
inside the concrete bunker.

And the unspoken:

When the shouting is silent
and the face is smiling,
when the shouting is hidden
and the face is smiling,

when the silence is shouting
and the face is smiling,
when the hidden is shouting
and the face is smiling,

when the shouting is smiling
and the face is hidden,
when the shouting is smiling
and the face is silent,

then the game is on.

And again, finding words for what I was seeing:

If I walk around in my blanket
I won't really have left my bed,
if I walk around in my dreaming tent
I'll manage, being half-awake and protected.

If I walk around in my blanket
the world won't open right up,
it won't ambush me with its full light,
I'm awake but still in dark's lap.

Half way there is as much as I can bear,
not too much world and all that shit,
so I come half way to what's there,
I walk around in my warm blanket.

From what I was picking up from users and from what was happening to me, I came to feel the ambivalence:

I'm addicted to the edge, call me back, call me back,
call me back to the centre, let me go.

I'm shivering in the wind, let me in, let me in,
let me come into the warm, let me out.

I think I've got a story, listen, listen please,
please listen to my story, go away.

I'm angry with the world, calm me down, calm me down,
calm my whole body down, just let me shout.

I'm going to shout, I'm going to shout, I'm going to shout,
    shout, shout,
I'm going to disappear up my own small voice.

I want you to help me and I want to carry on
being edgy, being mad, being exactly who I am,

because I'm crazy,
and I want to be crazy,
don't bore me with your cure,
don't tell me you're quite sure
who I am, what I want, what I need to be,
just leave me at the edge
because I'm crazy,
because I'm crazy
and I like it that way.

    The following I wrote for a young woman. I wanted to find a way of speaking her truth while also putting it away, letting the poem instead of herself bear it. This sounds overweaning, absurd even, but I did have sometimes a feeling that if what was experienced and told could be accepted (by me) as a gift, it might be given back—shared—as a poem, purposefully:

Walking the red line

The view isn't much to write home about
and home isn't much to write home to,
and the red line is hard to walk.

But red is roses and saints' days,
red is festivals and the glorious sunset,
red is a ripe picnic apple.

The past isn't much to make claims for
and the future is a long blank space,
and the red line is hard to walk.

But red is a Valentine heart,
red is the carpet rolled out for me,
and red is a ripe picnic tomato.

The soul seems homeless in this body
and the body feels homeless in the world
and the red line is hard to walk.

But red is a balloon in a clear blue sky,
red is one amongst the rainbow's many,
and red is picnic strawberries and cream.

Red is every kind of wound that hurts,
red is the fire that burns out of control,
red is blood that runs, runs, runs away,

and red is a butterfly doing its butterfly thing,
red is is the lips of a friend smiling,
and red is a cherry on a picnic cake.

There came a point when for my own wellbeing as well as for what I felt I was able to do as Poet in Residence, I needed a clear affirmative. I couldn't celebrate the ward, but I could and did write a crying out, a hopefulness, a statement of intent:

What I want is a safe place
where there's something that tells me
there's better to come
than I've yet known.

What I want is a bright place
that tells me something is possible
I haven't yet
discovered in my own life.

What I want is a truthful place
that tells me that the best I've known in my life
is real
and might be possible again.

What I want is a loving place
where what sparkles is real
and what hurts
isn't everything.

What I want is a playful place
which reminds me I could play once
and that one day with ease
I can play again.

What I want is a possible place
that shows me *possible,*
that is my *possible*
in a possible that connects.

What I want is a place that reminds me
of something much better
than I've been able to find
in my gone-wrong life.

What I want is some clear indoor air
so that I can breathe again
as if breathing matters
and is wonderful.

There were during the residency extraneous moments. I was invited to contribute to a poetry and prose reading, and to run a workshop, at the annual conference of the Royal College of Psychiatrists, that year at the Queen Elizabeth II Conference Centre in London. I read various of the above, and also wrote one or two specially, including this following, written during that week, after seeing a Van Gogh painting reproduced for PR purposes by a drug company:

Poor Van Gogh

What poor Van Gogh needed
was a little pill,
or perhaps not that pill
but a different little pill,
or perhaps a different one again
for a month, for a year, for life,
or perhaps a combination
of little pills, try this one, try that one,
try that one and another together,
lots of little pills perhaps he needed,
a thousand pounds' worth,
ten thousand pounds' worth,
half a million pounds' worth
given the research costs
and the cost of Public Relations
and the expectations of shareholders,

then poor Vincent could have
given up painting masterpieces
and vanished without trace
into old age.

And in Birmingham I was invited by the novelist Penelope Farmer,
who was creatively researching there, to do something informal at a
long-stay ex-hotel. We were having lunch in the dining room when a
man appeared, stood up straight in front of me and said, 'I won't be
writing a poem today, thank you.'

This struck me as curiously profound, perhaps very clear-headed
indeed, and it led me to write, as it were, his poem:

Not today, thank you

I won't be writing a poem today, thank you,
the trees are in the wrong place
and what we had for breakfast was too starry.

You know how it is, a poem has to grow in a box,
only not in any sort of box, I'm thinking to name red
or purple-green if there's rain, I found a poem once

that was trombone-coloured, and I can tell you
that one positively flew. Mine tend to be extranean
and best done on a pilot light, you will understand

like a dowry how this is done, oh the terrible arrival
of the messenger across the table, reaching, reaching,
and not reaching me at all, it slags my head.

Today I'm not in for any of that, today's to be quiet,
no bending the ear to any boom-boom or numb notes,
no minor keys, like spaghetti, all over the place,

and a twilight walk in the breeze of a fallow field,
I don't want any of that today, no thank you.
You're the kind of mad bugger that gets me going,

sticks your flute in my guts good and proper,
sets me diving for recidivist treasure, it's there,
oh yes it's there, jewelled cases of it, jagging my jugular,

tearing out my tent pegs, and I've only this minute
stuck those bastards back in. Now where am I to go,
no bloody tent, no field even now the storm's come,

and what do you care? A fucking poem then is it!?
I'll give you a fucking poem! Get me the music stand,
get me that beautiful music stand, silver, arms out,

I'll hang it by the neck till it's dead because it has
done nothing to deserve that. Fuck you, my friend,
I won't be writing a poem today, no thank you.

There is something surreal about the whole enterprise—who we
are, what this mental health 'sick' means, what 'balanced' means, what
kind of language is needed to enable us to rise to the extraordinary
while not 'going off the rails', if that is what we want. I wish I had
chased the surreal more conscientiously. Like this:

The ward now coming in to land

The ward now coming slantwise in to land
is running twelve melons early,
anyone meeting this ward
is advised it is very juicy
and may slide off the runway
into the bog seven miles away,
where the mermaids are still struggling
to get out of the story.
                    Regulations say
a juicy ward landing without permission
has to lose its tea trolley as ballast
and take off again, unless the mermaids
are staying and singing their fruit bowl song.
Please await further announcements.

And perhaps this, though it seems now a rather obvious listing:

Naming the corridors

This corridor we call *Tossing the coin*,
and this one is *Saying your prayers*,
this corridor is *Dark Lane*

and leads to *Imploding Stairs*,
this corridor we call *Mindful of your Fate*,
and this one remembers the dead
who fell in all the world's wards
and is called *Avenue Without Trees*,
this corridor is called *Deaf Alley*,
there is no breeze,
this corridor is short and goes on for ever,
we call it the *Straight Moat*,
we swim in it or float
or fall in
and are not known again by our real name,
this corridor is called *Way Out*
because it is, man, if your luck's in,
this corridor, where we meet angels,
is called *Silly Grin*.

Perhaps nowhere was more surreal than the chapel—a small, square, set-apart room—on a Sunday morning. I was glad to be there, and wrote this:

The chapel has chairs around three of its walls,
it's a square white room.
Along one wall this morning Ian and Danny
and the man who has seen Jesus
and along another wall the women who have seen a lot of years
and along the long window wall and in corners me and a few others
and the warmly-smiling nurse
and Bob's wife at the keyboard,
and Bob in his wheelchair handling the body and blood.

There's plenty between us to pray for and for each other
and I think we do, ask blessings each for each,
and we sing the hymn in several upon several modes—
always there's *Guide me O thou great Jehovah*, and
always afterwards Bob says,
'Cardiff Arms Park would be proud of you'—
Ian and Danny and the man who has seen Jesus,
and the women who have seen a lot of years,
and the warmly smiling nurse,

and me and the others and Bob's wife at the keyboard,
and Bob in his wheelchair handling the body and blood.

This is the place to be on a foggy Sunday,
with Ian and Danny and the man who has seen Jesus,
with the women who have seen a lot of years,
with me and the others and Bob's wife on the keyboard,
and the warmly smiling nurse,
and Bob in his wheelchair handling the body and blood.

We are not alone,
the storm has blown up in all of our secret lives,
'All hell has broken loose'—as the Gospel says—
and we hope to wake Him now with the words
off our little white sheets
and with the sighs in our little red hearts
and there's Peace—'be with you and with you and with you'—
and still within the storm—well, look at us—
there's a moment's something else

for Ian and Danny and the man who has seen Jesus,
for the women who have seen a lot of years,
for me and the others and Bob's wife on the keyboard,
for the warmly smiling nurse,
and for Bob in his wheelchair handling the body and blood.

When I began the residency I wondered about the varieties of language: that of the psychiatrists, of the psychologists and therapists, of the ward staff, of the social workers, and of the patients and their families. I wondered in what ways poetry was there already, to be found. And I encountered the managerial language, out of which, after a board meeting, I wrote this parody:

> If I can drill down
> into the core of this poem and
> hearing there the cacophany of voices
> somehow touch base with someone else—
> with you, with you—
> stay on track if the track is clear,
> and if for my short term goal I vere off
> into a ditch then I shall hope proactively to

bounce an idea off myself and
dig who I am if I am out
and be back on track, keeping my feet firmly
on the bottom line, staying alert
for leverage, and if I can get a handle on
the verticality
begin to come up for air,
unpacking as I rise the baggage accumulated
from my inner major players,
swim up through the logorrhœa
and meet the sun
coming on board
for another day's
articulation
of affection.

And, finally, a song for the deaf. My time in the unit for the deaf was another kind of education: conversations—and giving poems back in their own or in my voice—through signing interpreters and typed-up, watching television with sub-titles, and wondering what poetry is without sound. It occurred to me to write a song, which I did, for which a senior member of the nursing staff wrote the music. It was first performed communally, loud from a CD, led by a member of staff, with everyone—staff and patients—singing and signing.

I can see the shine

CHORUS:
I can see the shine in your bright, bright eyes,
I can see the shine,
I can feel the warmth in your strong, strong heart,
I can feel the warmth.

Here we go
bopping along,
here we go
singing this song.

CHORUS

Where to go
bopping along.
where to go
singing this song?

CHORUS

Somewhere to go
bopping along,
Somewhere to go
singing this song.

CHORUS

This we know,
we're bopping along,
we're on our way
singing this song.

CHORUS:
I can see the shine in your bright, bright eyes,
I can see the shine,
I can feel the warmth in your strong, strong heart,
I can feel the warmth.

Corridors, Stairs, Lifts

From a residency in Heartlands General Hospital, Birmingham

Here a bit soon and ticking over OK
In the Ante-Natal Unit

In and around
the little beds and the incubators—*Year 2000 compliant*—
a blue teddy bear, a yellow sea horse,
a red hippopotamus, a white duck in a blue hat,
no smaller most of these furry creatures than the babies
who one day will recognise and name and play with them.

The place feels holy—friendly holy, capable holy,
                attentive holy, no-hassle holy,
                clinical holy—in the presence
of the great mystery.
                A woman aged perhaps 70
walks past along Bordesley Green East scratching her nose,
a man aged perhaps 65 crosses at the lights,
a man perhaps 75 is walking his dog,
a 68 bus comes by half full,
an airliner is rising from the airport into cloud,
while inside this room the first little squeaks and cries of life
ask, 'What's this? What's going on?'

Sometimes a little hand comes up, waving,
then settles again slowly down: *It can wait.*

Tiny twins are newly in,
the first making a good healthy noise,
the second all right, it seems, but no sound yet.

It's the staff here really who have the poems
wordless inside them, and the babies
whose neo-natal experiences will be forgotten
while known for ever as poems in their inner nests.

Of course when they say

For the porters

Of course when they say fetch sharps, shrouds, body bags;
when they say fetch vomit bowls and bedpans, I do it,
when they say wheel a patient from A&E to X-ray,
when they say stand by for an accident coming in, I do it,

I know the length and breadth of the place, I know its walls,
I know its corridors, stairs, lifts, abrupt turns, its arguments,
I know its talk, its spleen, the heaviness of the afternoon,
I know the variance of smiles and winks, the stares, squints,

the years of learning, I know them, the talking briefcase,
the way the stethoscope hangs, I know it, the white coats,
the everyday clothes that are the supreme uniform, I know
the ranking voices, I know them, and the plaintive voices

of impatient, unpatient, opatient, ahpatient, starepatient,
griefpatient, dulledpatient, strifepatient, forlornpatient
waitingpatient, silentpatient, hurtpatient, lostpatient patients,
I pass by them, I wheel them, I move them, I am not them,

I am in control of, in charge of, responsible for no computer,
but I am present invisible on everyone's rolling screens,
of course when I am told, fetch sharps, shrouds, body bags,
wheel this patient to X-ray, take this blood to haemotology,

take a break, please don't take a break, be ready, take it easy,
fetch vomit bowls, shrouds and bedpans, bring more palettes,
move what was yesterday a warm person and is now a corpse,
wheel a trolley, pull a bed, be invisible, stand by, I do it.

The politics of sanctuary
The Infectious Diseases Unit

The politics of sanctuary
matter to me
and to be treated kindly
and to be here wholly

and to have love reclaimed
falteringly,
to have love named
openly

today,
let's say,
tomorrow
and, with something to show,
the next day
and the next.

I ask the poem
to speak plainly
and it looks back at me
and replies gently

that it knows nothing except
what I
surrendering
give it to say.

In the drift of torn
to take turn's hand,
open the wound's rift
of difference,
on the loose raft
of difference,
to take turn's hand then
is hard graft
in need of blessings
yes.

Turning is not tamed tribulation,
but out of good sleep
to wait
like a dancer on point
then move
into a flamboyance of response
between what has been
and what can be
eloquently.

Every living thing
has its right to try to be.
The pig that is now
in the ham sandwich.
The tree that is now this paper.
The spider that this morning
walked across my kitchen floor.
And me—
look at me, I'm here!
And the virus
which, establishing its right,
moves in on us.
It's all a matter of negotiation,

Turning is not tamed tribulation,
but out of good sleep
to anticipate
like a dancer on point
then move
into a flamboyance of response
between what has been
and what can be
eloquently.

Every living thing
has its right to try to be.
The pig that is now
in the ham sandwich.
The tree (O lovely tree)
that is now this paper.

The spider that this morning
sulked across my kitchen floor.
And me —
look, I'm here!
And the virus
which, establishing its right,
dances in on us.
It's all a matter of negotiation,
isn't it?

Here is the generator
and here is the cement mixer,
here are the men in hard hats,
here is the space for rebuilding,
here is a man carrying bricks,
here is a man carrying a bag of tools,
here are the cables, taps and joints.

What a disturbance,
what a noise,
what a business making the new map,
but now how good
to get the job done.

It was good, though,
and the memory,

who we were,
who we are,

the attraction then,
the *now* of always,

and not to be coy about it
the lovely fuck,

and pleasure still,
the mutual gift
yes.

                       This testament of tunes
                       all mixed up
                       so that longing,
                       grief,
                       merriment,
                       sadness
                       are all in there together
                       saying

                       this is how it is
                       and isn't, the truth of it,
                       the lie,

                       the harsh discords,
                       the sweet melody.

In the waiting area
HELLO magazine,
lots of them,

who
is wearing what,
where,
when,
with whom,
glittery
hetero-partners
glittery,
glittery
self-consciously opening their faces
for the camera.

                       At any time of year winter
                       is a steep climb, winter
                       is a dark room, winter
                       is scrag end.
                               O sweet sound
                       of spring song, O warmth
                       of summer calm, now
                       on these unnameable days,
                       please.

The cells joined

Written for the annual gathering,
arranged by the chaplaincy,
for relatives and friends after the deaths of babies

Words lost their meaning
and meant too much,
memory lost its grip
and had a hold never
to be released,
nothing was the same:
opening the curtains,
putting the kettle on,
dressing,
shopping,
hearing my own name,
and during the long night
the wait for nothing.
The cells had joined,
they had formed
and had tried hard.
The body had formed
and had tried hard.
The mind had formed
and had begun to know,
and had tried hard,
and had tried hard,
and had tried hard,
and had rested,
and had rested,

and rested

and rests.

Renal Unit Index

Admin sets
Air inline sets
Alco-wipes
All-Party Parliamentary Kidney Group
Ambulatory, and back
Anaemia
And how are you today?
Arterial line
Audit
Automated peritoneal dialysis
Auxillary . . .
Bag exchange
Baird's Bard Monopty biopsy instrument
Bandage
Baxter Cycler Drainage set
Baxter minicap with Providone-Iodine
Best do it, though.
Bleep, bleep
BL 834 Arterial Fresenius
Blood flow rate
Blood urea nitrogen
Blue aprons
Brown and blue needles
Butterfly needles
Care Assistant
CART Nurse
Chocolate biscuit?
Chronic renal failure
Cinbin for contaminated sharps
Cleaner
Clearance
Clinical Nurse Specialist
Clinical standards
Coach trip, anyone?
Coffee, thanks.
Community Liaison Worker
Community Nurse
Computer printout

Concentration
Connectors
Consultant
Continuous ambulatory peritoneal dialysis
Continuous cycling
Continuously cleaning the floor
Convulsion
Counselling Service
Creatinine
Cross-matching

Defibulator pads
Dermafilm
Diabetes National Service Framework
Dialysis
Dianeal peritineal dialysis solution
Disinfectant
Disposable tubing
Distant relatives
Doctor
Domestic Supervisor
Dry and itchy skin
Dry weight
Dulayse catheter

Edeme
Emergency
Excuse me, where's the loo?
Excuse me, where's the exit?
Excuse me, what day is it?
Exit site
Family
Flow meters
Fluid overload
Frekaderm alcohol-based disinfectant
Fresenius's bloodline tubing system

Gauze
Gerenal nephrology
Glomerulonephritis

Good afternoon, how are you?
Graft
Greetings from . . .
Granuflex
Green and orange needles

Haemodialysis
Handover meeting
Hello, how are you?
Hemoflow Fresenius Polysulfone
Heparin 1000
Heparin 5000
Here's a postcard from . . .
Here's an information leaflet, if you'd like one.
Hibiscol's rapid acting antimicrobial hand rub
Holiday
Home treatment
Hospal sterile and non-pyrogenic circuits
Housekeeper
House Officer
How do I do this?

I like it here.
I'm a friend.
I'm going to the canteen, do you want anything?
Indications
In the bowels of the ship the engineers
   and the stores
   and the pumping of water.
Intravenous
In-Tray
Isolators
It's a thought.
It's for you.
It's Tuesday again.
It's Friday again.
I've been trying to park.

Just in case.
Just popping out for a minute.

Kendall's Monoject syringe
Kidney Alliance
Kimal's fixed wing access needles
Large gloves
Last wishes
Let go.
Lignocane
Lovely bright morning.

Matron
Medipreps
Medical Student
Medium gloves
Melolin
Mepore dressing
Metallocene clinical waste sack
Metfix
Micropore
Mistakes
Monitor
Mouth pieces
Multidisciplinary team meeting

Nausea
National Kidney Patients' Helpline
Nebulisers
Nephrectomy
Nephrologist
Nephron
96 into town

On a roll
Only 53 emails this morning.

Patient Advocacy Liaison Service
Pen torches
Peritoneal cavity
Peritoneal dialysic record book
Phosphate binders
Plastiplak Biogel powder-free surgical gloves

Plastiplak sterile syringes
Please . . .
Polycystic
Presenius safe lock
Probe covers
Pruritus
PVC tape

Rational decisions
Receptionist
Registrar
Repeat list
Rocialle's Unicare renal pack

Sanitary towels
Scissor clamps
Secretary of State for Conditional Promises
Semipermeable
Senior Charge Nurse
Senior House Officer
Senior Registrar
Senior Sister
Senior Staff Nurse
Sink
Small gloves
Sodium chloride
Sometimes I wonder . . .
Staff nurse
Stay-safe disinfection cap
Sterets
Stopcocks
Student Nurse
Style-Plus drink cups
Suction hoses
Suction tubing

Tea, yes please.
Tegaderm
Thank-you.
There's a message for you.

Toxin
Transpore surgical tape
Transport in
Transport out
Treatment option

Ultrafiltration
Urea reduction ratio
Uremia

Venflons
Venous line

Ward Manager
Ward round
Waste
Well, good evening, how are you?
What day is it today?
What was that you said on Tuesday?
Where there's a will, . . .
White aprons
Who's for a coach trip?
Wide bore sets
www.kidney.org.uk

Year after year.

Zinc
Zip

My complaint
Customer Relations

Dear Customer Relations,
I wish to complain that your so-called complaints department
was so quiet this morning
and such a pleasant experience
I am having to go away calmer than when I arrived.

It's all very well knowing that in the past week
there have been somewhere on site complaints about
  toilets
  drunks,
  the décor,
  waiting times
  waiting times
  waiting times
  car park charges
  the cost of a small meal
  appointment instructions
  'the vending machine stole my money'
  security lights
  incontinence pads
  the height of chairs,
and a few compliments,
  'nurses are very kind'
  'excellent treatment'
  'extremely impressed',
and I dare say some clinical hiccups are being investigated
within 20 working days as set out in the complaints procedure
and I can see that your department
is a buffer between patients and Government,

but no one stormed in and demanded attention,
no one even phoned irate, done in, or over the moon.
What kind of a place is this, happy, relaxed, enjoying the work,
where's the drama in that,
what kind of a poem can you reasonably expect?!

Song of the Mapmaker

Text for a cantata of the Hereford Mappa Mundi

1. FOR THIS PICTURING

For this picturing I shall need
the whole skin of a calf,
a frame of oak,
deep black mineral ink
with soot or lamp-black mixed in
to make more intense the names,
the outlines and inscriptions,

and I shall need vegetable dyes,
red for the Red Sea and the Persian Gulf,
for some of the clothes, for the castellated towns,
brown ground to hold fast the paint,
olive brown for the route of the Exodus,
sepia for foundation,
mineral blue for lakes and rivers,
bright green for seas,
gold leaf for the largest capital letters
and for continents,
for cardinal points and for MORS—
for the firm frame of death and beyond
into the other worlds—

and a set of quill pens, from geese and swans.

2. THE WINDS

The twelve winds encompass us,
fork-tongued dragons surround us.

From the East at the top of my stretched skin
—Oriens where rises the great sun
and where Christ in majesty presides alone—

Vulturnus which dissolves and dries,
Subsolanus which hurls fierce showers,
Eurus, bringer of fatal disease.

The twelve winds encompass us,
fork-tongued dragons surround us.

From the West at my map's foot—
earth like my map is perfectly flat—
—Occidens where the sun will set—

Africus that conceives storms and lightning and thunder,
Favonius that ripens seeds, opens flowers, repents winter's vigour,
Chorus, cloudy then clear, all the winds together the great choir.

The twelve winds encompass us,
fork-tongued dragons surround us.

From the South at my right hand
where the Sciapod live, one-legged,
Meridiens the mid-day's winds,

Nothus, too hot, dissolves water out of stone,
Auster, humid hot, seduces flowers out of rain,
Auster-Africus, blows across from the unknown.

The twelve winds encompass us,
fork-tongued dragons surround us.

I shall write in the North at the far left,
Septentrio, a word flowing and soft,
the seven stars, the Great Bear's drift,

Circius, shaper and flinger of hailstones,
Septentrio herself, cold wind's dry star bones,
Boreas, who hoards clouds, holds their reins.

The twelve winds encompass us,
fork-tongued dragons surround us.

3. THE STRANGE CREATURES

Here will I draw the giant ants,
the ants that guard the golden sand,
they dig up gold and guard it well,

they dig up gold and guard it well,
the ants whose home is golden sand,

here will I draw the golden ants
the ants that guard the giant sand,
they live in gold and guard it well.

In Phrygia there's a Bonnacon
with curling horns and horse's mane,
when chased it shits three acres' worth
which burns when touched even through cloth.

The lynx sees through walls
and in its secret parts
produces a black stone.

I hope never to meet a salamander,
a most venomous reptile,
it is a newt with wings
and can live in fire.

The Mangradora plant
is most wondrously potent,
if you try to uproot it
it will shriek its head off.

Of course there are dragons at the far reaches
and some say they live under our very feet ,
they defend golden mountains I am sure of that,
the nearest ones I know of are in Wales.

It is said
of the crocodile
whose name is crocus

yellow like saffron
that once its teeth
have sunken in
it weeps
for its victim.

Their bones have been found,
the bones of Griffins,
their claws have been found,
the claws of Griffins
they have the bodies of lions,
the famed Griffins,
they have the wings of eagles,
the huge Griffins,
they clasp an Ox in their claws,
the fierce Griffins,
and are away into the skies.

Who has seen the Manticora
and lived to tell?
Who has seen its three rows of teeth
and lived to tell?
Who has seen its human face,
its bluish-grey eyes,
who has seen its lion's body,
its scorpion's tail,
who has heard its Siren voice
and lived to tell?

I have asked my friend with the steady hand
to draw for me the Phoenix, patient bird,
it lives for five hundred years, I've heard,
and only one is alive, only one of its kind.

I know no one alive who in truth has seen
the bird Phoenix plunge to its death in fire,
but I am sure it does, so says the tradition,
and rises again as bespeaking our Saviour.

4. THE MEDITERRANEAN

Sing the middle,   sing middle sea,
sing desert songs,   of the chosen people.
The gods of Greece,   the gods of Rome,
pillars of empires,   islands that breathe fire.

At the sea's neck   the Pillars of Hercules,
gods they said walked here   on Sandilitos.
Scilla's open jaws,   Charybdis's whirlpool.
In the Labyrinth   the hidden Minotaur.

Sing the tunny fish,   sing Sardinia,
sing the swordfish,   knight of the sea.
The fork-tailed mermaid   with her moon-mirror.
On the island of Rhodes   the Colossus.

At Alexandria   the wonder lighthouse.
On the Adriatic   the Delphic oracle.
Out from Delos   the world once spiralled.
At the Black Sea   the Golden Fleece.

Constantinople   on the crusaders' route.
At Minorca   they are sling-skilled.
Carthage for trade,   founded by Dido.
At Antioch   Jerome became priest.

Cairo an island   in the wide Nile.
Athens and Corinth   where Saint Paul was.
Sing desert songs   of the chosen people,
sing the middle,   sing middle sea.

5. THE PEOPLE AT THE EDGE HAVE THEIR SAY

I with my bird head had a song too
and I with my eyes in my chest
and I with one leg made a murmur
that was music to me at the edge.

I with no mouth but a small hole
sang in my bones and was heard
and I when I fought hard with griffins
came to rest with a whispering word.

So my head was covered in dog's fur
but I whelped with a tune to the wind,
my king had one eye in his forehead,
we grouped and sang songs with our mind.

We are fixed at the edge of the map now,
our difference is all that we have,
but ours was a beautiful song once,
a song in a beautiful trance.

6. CHRIST AND THE COMPASS POINT

When the point of the compass is set in its proper place
the very centre of the world is marked by the holy city.

Ligatures bind *mors*, death, to the world's outer rim,
there is no way round this rim than through Judgement.

Christ's arms on his Cross hold the whole world in place,
while triumphant in Majesty he sits at the outer rim.

Perfect circles can be drawn with the point in the tomb,
he is risen now and sits waiting at the outer rim.

Christ at the outer rim in Paradise clouded from us
raises his nailed hands and over the whole world presides.

Mary attended by angels opens her dress and her milk,
pleads for sinners whose devotions flow through her.

The trumpet is at the lips of the herald angel,
no one escapes judgement at the world's outer rim.

Everything revolves around Jerusalem the holy city,
salvation is from the centre where the compass works true.

7. J'INSCRIS LA FRANCE SUR LA CARTE

Par dessus la mer
de Normandie,
par dessus la mer
nous sommes venus construire

pour la sainteté
entourée pour le paradis
et quelques uns d'entre nous
sont venus de Paris,

cité des tours
dans l'air musical,
douce à l'oreille
et bien affilée,

par dessus la mer
nous sommes venus de France
changer la marée
du Saxon.

[I inscribe France on the map

Over the sea
from Normandy,
over the sea
we came to build

for sanctity
enclosed for heaven
and some of us
came from Paris,

city of towers
in musical air,
sweet to the ear
if sharp as well,

over the sea
we came from France,
turning the tide
of the Saxon.]

8. THE SMILING ANGEL CHOIR

I have watched the making of the smiling angel choir.
When they were fledged the King and Queen smiled here.
I have watched the making of the smiling angel choir.

Angels smiling sing *Laudate* to the trumpet and lute,
with pipes and cymbals they make perpetual praise,
they hold the sun and moon to let them freely shine.

I have watched the making of the smiling angel choir.
Queen Eleanor smiled when flying they fledged here.
I have watched the making of the smiling angel choir.

One angel not smiling expels Adam and Eve naked,
in one hand a sword, with the other pushing them out.
Until an angel smiles we are that same Eve and Adam.

I have watched the making of the smiling angel choir.
When they flew the king of castles Edward was here.
I have watched the making of the smiling angel choir.

King David has wings and holds ready his great harp,
an angel comes flying to the smiling Virgin and child,
Christ smiling reveals to a smiling angel his wound.

I have watched the making of the smiling angel choir.
When they were fledged the King and Queen smiled here.
I have watched the making of the smiling angel choir.

9. MY MISTAKES

I employed a man. I employed a man to copy my design on to vellum
and when I returned one day I discovered my words explaining
Abraham's city had become meaningless. Another day I returned and
there before my eyes were the words *artim ysidrus* which also were
nonsense, and so I remonstrated with the man who had done the
work, and afterwards to my confessor I conceded my anger and made
penance for it. Another day when the man had gone I saw where the

length and breadth of Africa was inscribed the word *longitudo* twice and it hurt my heart to see it. I corrected it as best I could. But the worst was to come with no means of redress or correction. I had already paid the man when I found the words *AFFRICA* and *EUROPA* entirely in their opposite places, crossed over, and my heart almost broke at it. So large were the letters and so filling the available space, I could do nothing but lie awake at night and endeavour in my mind's eye to exchange them into their proper continents. I cursed the man again and I cursed myself for my wanton negligence in explanation and oversight, and when I confessed this cursing my good Father in God admonished me but with a sigh, as if I heard him say, 'Jesus in his mercy understands your pain, my son, and will not hold it against you, but I understand there is in your picture a scroll in the hand of Christ on which are inscribed the words, *Behold my witness*. Repeat, he said, *Ave Maria* as many times as there are rivers on your map, and you shall be a faithful witness and blessed.' So I am reconciled but still heavy of heart every time I think of the mistakes, every one of them.

10. THE JOURNEYS OF THE EXODUS AND OF SAINT BRENDAN

Joseph had charge of the full barns of grain in Egypt
until on the second day of the Passover Israel departed.
Israel gathered in Rameses started its great journey.

Brendan in his small boat
set out across the wild sea,
from Ireland he set his sail
towards paradise.

For Moses leading the people the Red Sea opened wide,
the sea on their left and right was red as they walked through,
towards the Mountain of Sinai they were led then wearily.

Brendan in his small boat
sailing for a year of days
could see in his vision
the earthly paradise.

On the tablets of stone were written the *tabule testamenti*,
Moses received them from God in Heaven and he shone,
the horns on his head shone when he died and was earthed.

   Brendan found six islands:
   fields full of flowers,
   trees heavy with fruit,
   in unending daylight.

Astray in its thoughts Israel found an altar of gold stone,
and on the stone was an idol, weird with a wrangling tail,
their prayers to this idol flew in the air blind like flags.

   Six islands of Paradise,
   the islands of Brendan,
   blessed monks were with him,
   Saint Brendan we name him.

Israel through confusion journeyed by twists and turns,
the Jordan river that was to be holy was found and crossed,
the people of Moses came at last boldly to the promised land.

   Near the Atlas mountain
   I have marked the Canaries,
   here Brendan discovered
   the earthly paradise.

11. THE PICTURE OF BRITAIN

If Jesus our Lord came loving us in Britain
many weeks' march would have cruelly used him.

   The sea that spills
   over the far edge
   swills around us
   rude on all sides.

Never did he cross the narrow bridge to Scotland
nor on his way there see the glory of Durham.

The sea that spills
over the far edge
swills around us
rude on all sides.

Holy Wulfstan's Worcester must be shown
and my beloved Lincoln, river and high town.

The sea that spills
over the far edge
swills around us
rude on all sides.

London must be well marked and Canterbury nearby
and I'm putting Athur's Cadan in as reported to me.

The sea that spills
over the far edge
swills around us
rude on all sides.

Here's Cornwall where they speak their own tongue
not unlike Breton, facing west to the harsh ocean.

The sea that spills
over the far edge
swills around us
rude on all sides.

Wales of the wild Welsh where Edward's new castles
Caernaron and Conway keep them at bay from us.

The sea that spills
over the far edge
swills around us
rude on all sides.

Beyond is Ireland of the saints and beyond that
the dish of sea spills over so take fright.

The sea that spills
over the far edge
swills around us
rude on all sides.

Hereford must be added now, squeeze it in,
and spouting from Clee Hill the Wye and Severn.

The sea that spills
over the far edge
swills around us
rude on all sides.

12. THE SURVEY

As Luke tells us
a decree went out from Caesar Augustus
that the whole world
was to be described.

'Go into all of our world,
report to us what you find
on every continent,
come back and tell the Senate,
show this to everyone on demand,
my seal on this document.'

Nichodoxus,
Theodocus
and Policlitus
were sent.

Now I myself have described the world as I know it,
you who see my work or hear, on your way, report of it
pray to Jesus in his godhead for Richard who set it out
to be granted bliss in heaven when his time is set.

13. A VISION OF THE FUTURE

This morning of Saint Anthony,
hearing the cock shriek out
I woke sharply from a dream.
I had been startled
right out of my wits almost.

I saw news flying through the air
with no messenger attached to it,
I saw paper slid into a device
only to appear out of a device again
a hundred leagues away

and I saw myself looking back at myself
from a picture in a box
after I was dead
and I was moving still
and talking,

and I saw someone playing as if on a keyed instrument.
this time on the side of a box or casket
words appeared, appeared and were changed

and changed again and I saw the words on the box,
Mappa Mundi, and I saw the name *Richard of Haldingham*
and I heard music, I heard a choir singing my songs,

and I woke sweating.

Towards the line

—three—

The jigsaw of history has an infinite number of pieces
G8 Conference, Birmingham, 1998

When I was young, before Nixon and neither knowing nor caring
what NATO was or who ruled where or why or how, I hitch-hiked
far and wide and went on trips, often alone, sometimes two of us,
neither on business nor for politics, nor sightseeing nor for research,
but out of curiosity and, as my whole life has been, without clarity.

In Moscow we saw Lenin's body and in Leningrad Matisse's dancers,
worked in a summer camp in Ontario, washed up, cooked and jived.
Somewhere in the middle of the United States, late at night,
we were called out of a barn at gunpoint, hands above our heads—
there was someone on the run, and we'd been seen going in—

then taken kindly to two chalets—they insisted—for a safe night.
We heard Gene Krupa in New York and great bands in New Orleans,
saw totem poles in Seattle and rode horses in the Rocky Mountains.
Another time I walked that long, long road into Venice and bathed
in the exquisite air of St Mark's Square. In Rome the finger of God—

Michaelangelo's—stretched out to me, fleshy youth, and in Paris
feeling at home as I always have in unfamiliar places, I idled,
but didn't know Samuel Beckett was there or Picasso or Paul Celan.
Between Salonika and Naples I was sick on a crowded ship and on
to Pompeii. This and much else the bric-a-brac I carry with me.

In Munich I sang with my university choir in chapels and beer halls,
and later, on my own, hitch-hiking, found myself in Skopje
after the earthquake, through the crowds behind Tito's cavalcade
in some other Yugoslavian city, and on my way back from as far
as Petra and the Red Sea had my rucksack stolen off a train
in Belgrade. So, lifts up autobahns and repatriation from Rotterdam.

I have a half-Japanese niece and nephew, they've been here once,
I receive cards and photographs. We brothers were born in Wales
and our ancestry is in Essex and London's Mile End, near the docks.
It wouldn't surprise me to find our origins in Germany or Russia,
in Poland, the Pale, or wandering a millennium ago up from Spain.

Scoffing cakes
Manchester Cathedral, 1999

Me and the bishop were scoffing cakes
after the poetry prizegiving,
little iced ones and creamy ones.

Perhaps I thought, 'If he can I can,'
perhaps he thought, 'If he can I can,'
but I think we were both independently
little-cake addicts,
going back for another
and another,
and there were plenty left
just asking to be eaten.

Poetry had made us both hungry
for sweet things.

Communion is all very well
but plates of little cakes
have that something about them.

Let's say the roof of the cathedral had opened
as this manna was falling
and that all we were doing
was being grateful.

Eating chips with the saints
At Downpatrick, November 1999

This way to the floodlighting, ladies and gentlemen,
and this way to the Visitor Centre.

The world is collecting its winters and as we pass we collect ours,
floodlit some of them, some gently candle-lit, some fierce with fire,
some hardly visited by light at all.

This way to the illuminating manuscript, ladies and gentlemen,
and this way to the old plays.

I am eating chips with the saints after dark,
looking out over a town so lit up it must be someone's party here
      every day,
and the noise of traffic is constant, souls on their way.

I wonder if soul is renewed like skin, like heart, like other tissues of us
  after crying,
             after crawling, laughing, running, thinking, writing,
                crying,
         picking up the loose thread
      of soul-stuff.

No one gets a medal for bringing the festivities around again,
no command has brought winter on and the need for warmth,
when it reaches us we sing meaning at it and warm our souls.

I am eating chips with the saints after dark,
sitting on the great stone, half-believing conversation is possible,
laying a few chips on this cold stone,
not betting on it but here in the flesh
asking a blessing.

Our Lady is taking off with her child on a magic carpet.
Through her lowered eyes she will see
              the *shipwrightes* and *fysshers* and *maryners*
acting out the great flood.
              She will see the play change and change again,
she will see our world of floodlighting.

This way to the floodlighting, ladies and gentlemen,
and this way to the walls completed to be lit.

I am eating chips with the saints after dark in the roofless world,
at the edge of thought, turning over words.

Then in the twentieth century

Then in the twentieth century they invented transparent adhesive tape,
the first record played on Radio 1 was *Flowers In The Rain* by the Move,
and whereas ink had previously been in pots, now it was in cartridges.

They killed each other a lot and found ingenious and crafty ways to do it,
sometimes one person got killed, sometimes eleven, sometimes ninety-eight,
and some of the new equipment managed a million or more, it was, friends,

spectacular. Seymour, Foggy and Blamire gave audiences week by week
a chuckle, between 1941 and 1958 the New York Yankees won the world series
ten times, I did my A Levels, failed Physics twice, got Chemistry and Zoology,

and cycled a lot and drew maps. C. Day Lewis wrote a poem, *The Tourists*,
and George Steiner said, 'We must all learn to be guests of each other,'
I decided, in making my own poems, against punch lines, and lost in stages all

of my upper teeth. Peter Sutcliffe in 1987 confessed to thirteen murders,
when I was young we had no television, but we did have ice cream in cones.
Redundant churches became clubs, community centres, galleries or homes,

the phrase 'The best thing since sliced bread' (or not) got into the language,
Sir Basil Spence won the competition to build the new Coventry Cathedral,
I was born by the sea then lived in cities, Matisse in his old age made cut-outs.

One afternoon at precisely four-twenty, on the corner of Corporation Street,
wearing old jeans and a new red jacket, sheltering in a doorway from the rain,
she saw easily a man stab another man to death, blood everywhere.

Men quarrelled about scrolls found in pots near the Dead Sea, the library
at Norwich burned down, milk was pasteurised by law, I have four children,
all adult now, small islands became uninhabited, Harpo never spoke on film.

Ah

At a reading by Tadeusz Rozewicz at The University of Warwick,
May 2001

At the opening words of the poem
a woman in the audience raises her hand
half way, turns it slightly,
leaves it there.

There are more words, her head
is to one side,
she lowers her arm.

There are more words, her arm seems to
shiver by itself.
She smiles.

There are more words,
she opens her hands.

A till receipt poem, 2001: the truth

At 14.04 on October 1st
in the Food Store in Aldeburgh
I bought tomato purée, red pesto,
drinking chocolate, fromage frais,
fat-free milk and a plate tart.

At 11.36 on October 11th
I bought a copy of the Guardian
in the Stowmarket Tesco's.

At 9.08 on October 16th
in Holland & Barrett in the Pallasades, Birmingham
I bought two packets of sugar-free mints.

At 17.29 on October 17th
at HMV in High Street, Birmingham.
I bought a Rossini *Stabat Mater* CD.

At 14.27 on October 23rd
at Superdrug in Walsall
I bought a packet of sugar-free mints
and a packet of sugar-free chewing gum.

At 13.35 on October 24th
at the Warwick University Arts Centre Café Bar
I bought a pot of tea.

Here
In Aberdaron Church, May 2001

Any hand-held pulpit
has a scenic view,
a landscape of eyes,
a movement of hands,
the shifts and sways of bodies.

This one has also the sea through windows,
it has the slab-stones of sea-sung bodies,
it has sea-peeled walls,

and close up
as if about to interrupt the flow
here's the path. With the door open
children might,
holiday-makers might,
poets might,
the familiar might,
the strange might,
the disgruntled and the joyous might,
Jesus might
pass or come in.

Top ten benches 2002
For Rosemary Tolley

1. Mullion Cove, Cornwall
2. Worcestershire Beacon, Malvern Hills, Worcestershire
3. Courtyard, Saint Michael's Mount, Cornwall
4. The churchyard, Breedon on the Hill, Derbyshire
5. Waseley Hills Country Park, Worcestershire
6. Pendennis point, Falmouth, Cornwall
7. The graveyard, Jordan's Quaker Meeting House, Buckinghamshire
8. My garden, Kings Heath, Birmingham
9. Fox Rosehill Gardens, Falmouth, Cornwall
10. Top of the cliff, Dunwich, Suffolk
11. Saint Anthony in Roseland, Cornwall

Ten best doors 2003

1. Glass swing doors, MAC Hexagon room, Birmingham
2. Room 542 English/ Humanities, University of Warwick
3. My new back door, after the burglary
4. Double doors, old building, Lifelong Learning, Selly Oak, Birmingham
5. A door in the Forest of Dean
6. Front door, Sacrista Prebend, Southwell
7. A door in Rickmansworth
8. Holly's acupuncture door, Moseley, Birmingham
9. Double doors, Summer School, Continuing Education, University of Warwick
10. The door to the writing room in the Undergraduate Building, Heartlands Hospital, Birmingham
10a. A car door, Cornwall

Crossing
For Roy Fisher, 2003

I have come to where the Rea trickles
under the Birmingham & Worcester
at Lifford,
   the one named for itself, the other
for what could be shifted for hard cash, the one
on its long way to the sea, the other merely
tweaked this way and that by a breeze,
   the one in its deepest cut,
   the other superficial, flat.

On the cut's bank a rusting shell of a car
left here by Offa; along the surface water
a tripper chugging to Gas Street and wherever
the brochure said was picturesque.
A single rope and log swing is tangled
around the branch of a sycamore:
Dare you, then, over that steep slope.

I hold high the fisher man's *Birmingham River*,
I hear *Yes* and a chuckle and a chord or two,
and into the dark of the tunnel syncopation
that will emerge into the light again as a tune
towards Digbeth and Eastside
where the City plan shows the new library.

     Birmingham River
is ambivalent, says,
I like it *here*: the rough cut, the brambles, nettles,
shadows across smoothed stones.

Itch, cram, britch and ratch

Poems of Birmingham

The Bull Ring

1.
The Bull Ring is coming down,
the Bull Ring is coming down,
piece by piece it is coming down,
day by day a bit more of it comes down,
a bit more of the Bull Ring comes down,
every day a bit more of it.

The Rotunda is staying up,
the Rotunda is staying up,
piece by piece it is staying up,
day by day none of it is coming down,
every day the Rotunda is staying up,
every day all of it.

The Ring Road is being torn up,
the Ring Road is being torn up,
inch by inch it is not a road any more,
day by day it becomes less of a road,
cones show temporary ways through,
new ways through change to other ways through,
every day more of the road is no road at all.

Look at that rubble, the rubble that was the Bull Ring,
where rubble is, the Bull Ring was,
where there were clearly defined walls
now there is rubble,
where we used to shop and go up and down escalators
is every day more rubble than Bull Ring,
every day more of it is waste,
waste is what it now is,
look at that rubble, last month it was Bull Ring.

The Rotunda is not being pulled down,
the Rotunda is not becoming rubble,
piece by piece it is what it always was
since it displaced the rubble of what was there before it,
day by day none of it is coming down,

every day the Rotunda is staying up,
every day all of it is still called Rotunda,
none of it day by day is becoming rubble.

But the Bull Ring is coming down,
the Bull Ring is coming down,
piece by piece it is coming down,
day by day a bit more of it comes down,
a bit more of the Bull Ring is coming down,
every day a bit more of it.

2.
Between the knocking down of the old Bull Ring
and the building up of the new Bull Ring
there was a wonderful big hole,
there was a wonderful big hole
like a Welsh quarry
or a place hit by a meteorite
or a mountain turned inside out.

A child would go to school and say,
'Have you seen the hole, Miss?!'
The word went round, 'You've got to see the hole,'
so that Mums and Dads got taken there
to wonder at this great Birmingham treasure,
the big hole.

Where did it go, the big hole?
Where did it go, that precious big hole
with the walkway over it,
so that from the walkway we could look far down
into the big hole,
so that our legs went wobbly
looking down at the big hole,
where is it now? The word
surely went around the world,
'See Birmingham's big hole.'

And they'll be coming from across the world
by air,

by train,
by car,
on foot,
asking, 'Where's the big hole?'
And we will have to say, 'Sorry, you missed it.
It was here,
now it's not here any more.'

3.
The Bull Ring is going back up,
the view that was downwards is upwards again,
purple carbuncles and glass are going up,
the new Market Halls are up, up already,
St Martin's has it's gold cross back up, up,
a massive new Debenhams is up, up
and will open SOON, SOON, SOON.

The Bull Ring is going back up:
Over 130 exciting new stores,
3,000 new parking spaces,
open till 8pm 6 nights a week,
it's all numbers there now in the Bull Ring,
the Bull Ring that is going back up, up, up.

In some cities the up is towards a mountain,
some cities rise to a view of the ocean,
some cities rise to a great park.
We have at the top of the up, up, up some concrete blocks
that would have done old Romania proud.
Not the Capital of Culture, but of litter
and of King Kong long gone,
and of a Bull Ring that is going up, up, up.

City where you can sit in your car in traffic jams,
city where you can sit on a bus in traffic jams,
city where you can cycle at your peril in traffic jams,
city where you can walk and die slowly of exhaust poisoning,
and eventually reach the new Bull Ring
which as I write is going up, up, up.

4.
Once the Christians of Saint Martin's
tried to drown out John Wesley with bells
as he preached in the Bull Ring.
Such a magnifcent peal,
against one man's
market-place convictions.

Now the spire of the ancient church,
mausoleum of the *de Berminghams*,
is a set-piece picturesque
for the new store-land, European
City of Stuff.

Timetable

From Euston's Doric
to Birmingham's Ionic Curzon Street
1838
in five hours
the new religion of railways
was something to take tea by
along the route,
grit in your eye
as *Hercules* goes by
at, believe it or not, 20 mph:
'I saw it!'

Then it was two-and-a-half hours 1854
Euston to Birmingham New Street's
broadest span roof in the world, glass.

Now the new Virgins through New Street
have replaced the old Virgins and

at Moor Street
             the train now standing at platform 2
is running sixty-four years late.
This is due to an Einsteinian blip
between Aberystwyth and Shrewsbury.
We apologise for the late running of this train,
we hope that the coffins, wheelchairs, walking sticks
and flasks of Bovril
have been helpful, we would like to
apologise for the inconvenience caused,
and to welcome you to the 21st century.

Spaghetti nature

There is much to see and revere here, Desirée,
perch, bream, carp and roach.
As the roar goes by, my dear Desirée,
breach, cream, reek and lurch.
All in the lake, Desirée, dear, to be hooked,
itch, cram, britch and ratch.
Just then something jumped, really leapt, Desirée,
crutch, croom, patch or retch.
Wishing you were here, Desirée, wishing you were here.

The nettles need dusting, the campion, too, Desirée,
and the broom, the cow parsley and the wild mustard,
and the oat grass as well, and the vetch and the dock,
the dandelions need dusting, Desirée, and the brambles.
So much bright yellow, and the greens, the groans,
the reegs, the porslay, the brim, the wilt misted,
and the oot gross, and the votch, and the dack,
ond the dondiloons, all need dusting, and the brimbles.
If you could see, Desirée, the brom and the itch,
the willed mostord, the urt griss, the drimbles,
the wanderloons, the dak, the attles, the ompion.
Wishing you were here, Desirée, wishing you were here.

I know you are weary and beautiful, Desirée,
far away in your winsome glade,
but if you were here you could see the grebe nesting,
you could hiss back when it hisses,
you could quack back at the ducks,
you could squawk at the lone seagull,
you could be silent back at the coots,
for believe me if you strain your ears
these things can be heard,
the grobe hossing, the gall squakking,
you can hear the quock of the dack,
the ilonce of the coost, all lovely,
all doing their own thing in their own way,
squicking, sclooting, whasking, grobe-hussing,
stook-shisshing, lig-squikking.

O yes, Desirée, I wish you were here, my dear,
I wish you were here.

Perhaps the great pillars support a temple, Desirée,
perhaps in their curving lanes Cadbury's and the Royal Mail,
lorries full of beds, and vans full of forget-me-nots,
do their trips and twirls, their roundels and winks,
on this axis, on this great wheel, on this celestial compass
for the greater purpose.

Desirée, if only you knew what goes on here without you.

Birmingham & Black Country industry

Canal construction
retaining enough water in the upper reaches,
constructing locks and tunnels in the 1770s   Put the kettle on,
and 1780s the canals circuitous and narrow.   Bill.
Cheap transport after the inadequacy of packhorse
road transport even with better turnpike roads.

Coal
iron
limestone   Cuppa tea, Tom?
clay
bricks
metal.

Iron smelted by coal.
The slitting mill.
Dry puddling.   Time for a beer,
The steam engine freed the iron trade   Enoch?
from the limitations of water power.

James Watt's single-action engine.
Partnership with Matthew Boulton   Pass the sherry,
and with William Murdoch.   James?
The SOHO works.

The Newcomen atmospheric engine.
Rotative motion.   Put the kettle on,
Sun and Planet motion.   Doris!

Industrial pottery, salt glazing, Devonshire   Im right dying for a
ball clay for white-bodied earthenware.   beer, I am, George!

Calcined flints.
Spode's incorporation of calcined bone.   Where's that tea,
Josiah Wedgwood.   Betty?!

The blast furnace. Iron, iron, iron.

The railway began to replace the canal,
except to a large degree bulk freight.

One pint down the
hatch, two pints—

Fashion, metal buttons, silver-plating.

Tea, dear?

The old hand-made nail trade undermined by
mechanisation.

Malleable iron, the blast furnace
and in the coalfield area 400 mines produced
72 million tons of coal each year.
Pig iron: 4 million tons each year.

Pint of mild and a
brandy.

Localised trades: tubes in Wednesbury,
nuts and bolts in Darlaston, hollow ware and
springs in West Bromwich, saddlery in Walsall,
locks in Wolverhampton.

And more tea.

Birmingham: a double acrostic

Brummagem in King Offa's middle lands, baB.
Imperial, European, off Junction 6 SpaghettI.
Rotunda around which the world spins, deaR.
Mooch the new Bull Ring, the blobs, gawp 'eM.
In secret be a Cadburyholic, drive an old MinI.
Not adjectivally a rosy city, keep yer'ead dowN.
Get to St Andrews or the Villa and get yellinG.
Hoot the canals, sing the little rivers awasH
Agin the meres, crofts, leats, vales and leys A
Merry Hobbit's haunt is Birmingham, maM.

Remember marjoram

Remember marjoram for blushes,
remember harebell for grief,
throatwort for beauty neglected,
blue convolvulus for repose,
pennyroyal for fleeing away,
dark geranium for melancholy,
sweetbriar eglantine for poetry—I wound to heal—
red catchfly for youthful love,
witch hazel for a spell,
aspen for lamentation,
hawthorn for hope,
remember crimson polyanthus for the heart's mystery,
remember rosemary for remembrance,
and applaud this little yellow flower
coming up through the concrete
and waving.

Haydn comes to lunch
& sends a letter home

The Coull Quartet plays Haydn's opus 33 no. 2
in the Philosophy Department Common Room,
University of Warwick, at lunchtime, March 2002

My love, I am in Philosophy
    and am encountering
        garlic dip
        plain crisps
        spicy crisps
        crisp rings
        spicey dip
        red wine
        bottled water
    and these ideas are tasty, such an illusion of taste
    I might almost have imagined I am enjoying
    the real thing.
                I think my quartet now
    and off it goes.

i. *Allegro moderato, cantabile*

What should we wear so as to have interesting thoughts?
    What should we wear to stay close and hear?
        What do shirt sleeves bring on, what a pleated skirt?
        Socks, shoes, abandon them? I imagine

a Bb heater disrupting my Eb major,
              a C# whine in the wall,
    snoring in discordant fifths. Thank Gott
        no one drops the sounds *wine glass*

while my tunes do their turns.
              Mr Wittgenstein enters
              at bar sixty-three
    asking in a loud whisper for a spoon,
        then seeing a pen on the floor laughs

and takes it. Even philosophers die, my dear,
        there are signs and the cusps of signs,
anniversaries for remembrance, *O mein Gott*, forgive me—
    the day we saw each other deep in the eyes—
    I shall explain to you the arrival and departure lounges
    in this modern world
            and their revolving doors.

ii. *Scherzo. Allegro.*

Let's attempt a different dance,
　　let's dance a different attempt,
　　　　let's attempt the thought of a dance,
　　　　　　let's dance an attempt at thought,
　　let me tempt you with a different kind of turn,
　　　　let me turn you, let me swing this argument
　　for a quite new tempt, a twinkle of a new thing
　　　　　　　　　a trifling thing
　　to keep you awake, so
　　　　　　　imagine yourself
　　　　　　　　　　　　in love
　　　　　　　　on the turn
　　　　　and it's fun.

　　　　　So what if a soul feels strange
　　　　waiting at the door of nonsense
　　　　　　holding the line between
　　　　knowing and dumb? Can *blue*

be the same word
　　for the sky through the window
　　and for the CD cover
　　　of the quartets of this fellow
　　Schubert? I hear

a professor
left out in the rain
　without benefit of filing cabinet,
　of brown envelopes, brown folders,
　without comfort of hard disc and software,
　without tickle of phone? O but I must lose myself
　in my cool quartet—
　　　　　　　wicked, a student says, puzzling me.
　　　Let's,
　　　　　let's,
　　　　　　let's,
　　　　　　　let's go shopping for keys,
　　　　　　　for chords and cadences.

Where can I buy a juicy,
                        a juicy,
                                a juicy
        glissando,
                where can I buy the rules
                for the edge of language?
                Even Spike Milligan dies.

iii. *Largo sostenuto*

And in a leisurely way to wander through the brain looking for *theos,*
and to be prepared to defend your position against a fugue when the
moment is not right, and to flick up leaves with your toes in a forest
clearing towards an already scarred meeting, and no grass nourishes,
no flowers brighten, and poetry uses up transcendence always, and
let's go forward now to our very own problems of self, and because
philosophers die how should we think? And how different thought
is in a comfortable chair here in B*b* major, how silent the voices of
redundant books,

                but alert in that particular forest on that
                particular day with the problems of self
                promiscuously present and yet with the
                grass its usual self, but yet to call again
                for fresh language to be uncomfortably
                desirable, but yet in a clearing even
                philosophers need before long to eat, but
                yet the soul goes silent, but yet even voices
                in the asking, but yet if redundancy be
                found in our kind of time, but yet if fluency
                is to reveal its river of blessing, but yet if as
                seems inevitable we are to remain scarred,
                but yet one day when books, . . . but yet
                one day when a holy—no one here speaks
                of holy—fugue, but yet the glow of the
                turned river's *truth* may
                show itself as anything but
                light, but yet transcendence between
                glances, but yet pain, pain,
                pain, pain, pain,
                                using us up.

iv. *Finale. Presto. Joke.*

Mandelstam: 'Quick,
I've got it,
note it down!'

So here we go now
        neither leaving time behind
     nor going ahead of it,
       neither trying to tame time nor
      accepting its waywardness
           but tripping
      up and down the bar lines,
         a rush of adrenalin
      and off we go again,
a rush of fun and off we go again,
     get this piece out of the way soon,
      get on with something
        more interesting. One two,
one, two,
one, two,
  one, two, tickle my clue,
    three, four, surprise me more,
five, six, stir the mix,
   seven, eight, open the treat,
nine, ten, shut it again,
  eleven, twelve, shelve it!

     And now good friends I—

Do I have more notes? Can I can find them? If I can—

    Quick, I've—

So it's *danke* now and *auf wiedersehen*, a wave and—

   Quick, I've—

It's in my soul, this

Thorpeness, 2001

1.
These relentless—
it's in my soul this,

following-me waves, laughter-tidal-
tears-waves, bundling-
along waves, my soul
this,

makes me, breaks me,
look in the wind

poem—puny, stillborn, reckless,
too-sure—Oh

I could walk up and down the beach here
till I die, and be—

and be no more foolish,
and no more wise

than watching waves in a room
or scratching at pebbles brought home

in my coat pocket
that were rocks as the

big bang
cooled. With you here,

here would be different,
yes, different.

2.
I'm not naked enough to find my poem here,
I bring too much,
I have taken up occupation in myself
like concrete in a hole in the sand,
nor can I do it with prayer,
                         that lurch

to the *there* of *wherever*
that is not *here*.
                        Yet every wolf-wave
tries to tell me, each deep howl,
each lover-whisper, withdraw, show, whisper
and almost
I imagine
I can find it.

3.
It has something to do with semi-tones,
with disorderly chords, with a Suffolk minor key,
with tugging bass wrench,
        with a shift to a different minor, Welsh,
with anticipatory riven shifts.
        It has something to do with
the crunch-crunch of the stones, that
unsingable rhythmic.

4.
The ragbag I am
watching dragonflies copulating at speed
at the edge the movement called *cliff*
crumbling
between Thorpeness and Sizewell,
no rescue operation possible
only a sunny interlude.

5.
I photograph on the beach a yellow cone,
I photograph on the beach small slabs of brown crumbling stone
that might be a by-product of nuclear fission,
I photograph on the beach a newspaper left open,
all this is easy.

6.
O gull
who struggled twenty yards out
with an anchored hook in your mouth,
again and again easing your head into the sea

and yanking it out again,
who attempted take-off, opening your wings wide
only to have them fall back shut again,
who fought with *hook* and fought and fought.
I couldn't save you, could only watch
as one then another then a third gull arrived
and circled above you
then went. I'm sorry, I say now
the morning after
to your dead body, floating there still,
still, dead still.

7.
Open, bright, pure light here,
my dark place.

8.
I was wondering with the group
about our theatre of voices:
'I am son, brother, father, friend, poet,
and each of these further to be subdivided' —
I omitted *priest* but included it privately —
'I am lost soul' — and at this there was some laughter,
and I, too, smiled.

9.
Did you see that couple on the beach kissing?
No, you were hundreds of miles away.
I saw them.

10.
On the beach I have been constructing and arranging
with pebbles,
with sticks,
with a fragment of spine,
with an empty plastic bottle
where the tide will come in
and destroy everything I have made.
This, surely, is good Zen practice.

I have photographed what I made before the sea comes for it.
This practice is not so good.

11.
Along the path alone between Sizewell and Thorpeness
I reach my hands back behind my *self*
for you to hold.
                    Haven't I been advocating
again and again
the power of the imagination?

12.
Where the sun sets, round and round,
where it rises, round and round,
and return is impossible
except as thirst,
carrying my wares: this poem. This one, this one?

13.
Lords of limit
you have scrambled my vocation —

   voice — voice — sponge — gate — tide —
you have blessed and cursed me with strangeness,
and now I am to understand the trip-wire
is a form?

14.
How bloody painful
wonder
is.

15.
There is a ship out there in this autumn dusk,
its long block of itself,
its yellow light,
its red light,
a light at one end uncertain of its hold in air
as it were a candle
in the last days. I am standing square on to it,
and it, short of the horizon,
is square on to me and
in the morning when I open the curtains
it will have gone,
and soon after
my being here having seen it
will have gone too.

Towards the line

—four—

Cædmon's song and a translation

Nū scylun hergan   hefænrīcæs Uard,
Metudæs mæcti   end his mōdgidanc,
uerc uuldurfadur,   suē hē uundra gihuæs,
ēci Dryctin,   ōr āstelidæ.
Hē ǣrist scōp   ælda barnum
heben til hrōfe,   hāleg Scepen.
Thā middungeard   moncynnæs Uard,
ēci Dryctin,   æfter tīadæ
firum foldu,   Frēa allmectig.

Now we must praise   the measurer of heaven
convincing creator   great in thought
working glory-father   wonderful, strange
eternal maker   in the beginning decided.
First he formed   for the descendents of people
the sky-roof   this holy creator
then the earth   a good place for people.
Eternal maker   afterwards he made
people for the earth   the all-making maker.

Went for a walk

Eve of Remembrance Day, Symphony Hall, 2004

Went for a walk, saw a man crying by a tree,
asked him if I could help, he shook his head.
I hung around, he said, 'Leave me, please.'
I went for more walk. I get the news daily,
I hear what's happened, I'm still hereabouts
in my skin, in my shoes, in my small mirror,
through five-barred gates, through kissing gates.
It isn't beautiful a futile death. A poem doesn't
give a futile death meaning, only lays words on it
like dogdaisies on a grave, taken by the wind.
Perhaps the tree helped, knowing a thing or two
about comings and goings, about tears, wind.

Exile

Don't think of exile as a weed,
it is a beautiful flower,
if you believe it, it can provide milk.

Against the rules of exile, people
kill each other. I remember once I wore

the purple flower of exile
sticking out of my pocket
until it wilted, dried out and died.

Exile is not to be picked and put in a pocket,
nor even to be put in a vase.
Do not give it to a lover.

At the Abbey well

Let's meet one evening at the Abbey well,
I'm thinking we'll sing quietly at the Abbey well.

A body disintegrates in that silent place,
hear the bone's sharp ring down the Abbey well.

There is a man who knows exactly what's there
or seems to, when it's raining, at the Abbey well.

No one knows a monk who knew a monk who
knew a monk who drank long, at the Abbey well.

Natural water with minerals, still, by the bottle,
across borders, in places far flung, from the Abbey well.

Hear now the cry of the wounded, stricken hart,
here, here, precisely here, stung, at the Abbey well.

The stiltwalkers

For Miriam Obrey

We have come over ridges and across wide plains, through dark valleys,
we have found the course of streams, following ancient tracks.
Blown off course many a time, we who have known impatient wind
that urged us to fly, that interpreted us to air, that argued us away,
have come from a place of sweet, pure light into shadow, fright-darkened.

> We are the stiltwalkers, we have crossed the world,
> we are the stiltwalkers, we were loved by the wind.

We left behind the lazy swaying on their sticks, they watched us leave,
we left behind the sick on their stilts, leaning against trees, they watched,
the old on their sticks stayed, some of our best tilts and a shaman.

> We were restless, so we set out,
> babies on our backs, to cross the world,
> to find a new sacred place.
> We felt called by the wind to do it, our sticks
> our necessary stammer.

When we set out, our smocks were bright, we wore the sun and the moon
testing us. We were bright trees in our bright cloaks for our bright dance,
we were trees on the move, trees arriving at last to dance. The ghosts
of our past danced with us,
            the people we would become
                        danced in us, we flapped our arms
and we were prayer flags,
            the wind flapped, we were prayer flags,
our arms, our long coats, our scarves, our breaths, all were prayer flags,
            we were in love with the wind, the wind was in love with us,
the wind would unbalance us if it could, sometimes it did and we laughed.

A sparkle as we travelled began one morning to excite us all, and we giggled
            and fell all of us off our sticks into a pool almost
        in shadow, as if we were about to disappear deep inside ourselves,
    and be lost for ever. We were afraid. Giggling
        had been our faith, we were scared now. We entered

the terrible delay in which not one of us could say
yes to the way, yes to the pause, yes to thought,
there was no yes to plans,
our laughter turned sour, our stilts splintered.
What once was patient in us for the circle dance
into the onward dance into light in all weathers
has become mere agitation.
We want now,
we want to own ground, to own air, to own the best sticks,
we are sick with our own want.
We are
the empty playtime of the people we were once,
we ache for home and we have no home,
we believed in the long reach of our souls,
now our souls fray.
Where we lived there was a pivot of high ground,
we danced at the edge on every side
where one wind or another would provoke dance,
with the sun full on us,
we believed one day we would fly.

We are the stiltwalkers, we have crossed the world,
we are the stiltwalkers, we are loved by the wind.

Holy

the dance of the sticks. We used to dance. Our children
used to dance. Our children.
We had our own ground. We owned no ground.
We had our own air. We owned no air.

After the Party
February 1998, Walcot Hall

I am caught *in flagrante* with God
among the snowdrops,
the wind from the West is prematurely on heat,
the woodpecker says 'Knock it off,'
dead leaves which imagined they had come
to the end of their useful life
say they will support the match
with fiery crackling.

There has been a party,
heart-shaped balloons cling to the ceiling,
the room is full of empty bottles
each with its message.

I shall invent an old saying:
He who swims in the lake with God
will need no breakfast.
The lake is cool and calm,
the lake has trees in it upside down,
there is sky in the lake endlessly deep,
the lake holds a measureless kiss.
All the way from the snowdrops
and from the crackling of the dead leaves
and from the balloons clinging to the ceiling
and from the empty bottles
with their messages
is down hill.

Thus Valentine lost his head,
poor fool,
his head is the bell
that continues to toll
in flagrante with God
calling my wound
at the top of the hill.

The stone says and the sea does

The stone says, I shall be a brain,
the sea rubs away the cells,

the stone says, I shall have an eye,
the sea scoops it out,

the stone says, I shall be a skull,
the sea smoothes it away,

the stone says, I will have amber blood,
the sea swabs it white,

the stone says, I shall have a claw,
the sea dissolves it,

the stone says, I shall carry a map of the cosmos,
the sea wipes it into itself,

the stone says, I shall carry writing,
the sea can't reply for laughing,

the stone says, I shall bear the poem,
the sea is so tickled it can't even listen,

the stone says, I shall be sand,
the sea gives a victory roll,

the sand is heartbroken
trickling through my hand,
its voice gone.

Given

On the beach at Thorpeness, for Lizzi Thistlethwayte

If someone doesn't hold me tight I shall be blown away.
If I am blown away and all is forget, forgot,—

I am the argument from design.
I like a pot of tea by the lake.
I am with others here alone.

The eastern beach may meet the western beach one day
and I shall know my place anywhere.

You are my souvenir, my keep-keep,
my keep-keep, keep-keep.

What is given,
what is given freely,
what is given,
what is given as flow,
what is given whole
and taken away in pieces
examines me.

And keep-keep breaks apart—
the rules,
the rules—
keeping my clothes on,
keeping my excitement in,—

I am examined by keep-keep
and by let-let.

I am my own look-alike,
I am keep-keep and let-let.

The city will keep and let me
where God can't see.

The wave-risks, the truth-risks,
not only in poems but in the
loose folds
where I wait alone.

Keep-keep, let-let, the tide of it
without ease.

It's a cheap trick, this,
asking wide-open space to bless.

Such loose limbs the sea has,
I am in the drag of it and will
rust like a driftwood hinge.

Each moment I want now to live again,
to have that chance to let air in.

By a whim of the light the ship I saw
easing itself along the horizon had on the
navigator's table an envelope being held for
safe keeping with my name on it,
a poem for me in it
awkwardly sent.

Feldman says, if anyone asks

3.
And so,
if anyone asks, tell them the synagogue is closed,
soon it will be rubble, tell them,
worship here now is out of the question for ever, dust
for one thing, broken floor boards for another and rot.
If anyone says they have to pray tell them
to pray in the street or in the kitchen, well why not?
Everything is in perpetual change, tell them that,
they'll know it already, every day says it, tell them anyway,
some place, some other place, some other, other place,
say if they want to sing psalms do it with good grace
in the bath.
        I am
too old for this, I want a quiet life.
If anyone says they have a right,
tell them to speak to the Almighty, not to me,
the place was filled, now as obvious as a broken violin string
it is emptying.
        It was
stuffy anyway, reeked of good sense,
everyone was too happy here, too happy and now
there's just you and me and you only make-believe for warmth.
Soon there won't be anybody,
but if somebody asks please
say we are closed for lunch and tell them lunch this time
will last for ever, dear me I'm crying.
Do you see this, my friend, real tears?

7.
All kinds of people, people with names,
will gather round, believe me,
poking their eyes into the desolation,
hoping someone will provide a cup of tea.
Someone nearby will be sucking a carrot,
children will be playing with guns.

9.
Here is a man pushing a synagogue
on a wheelbarrow, round and round.

The bones in the synagogue in the wheelbarrow
sing the holy song for the last time
and again for the last time
and again.
     When the wheelbarrow stops
and the man pushing it is collected up
he will be pressed in a book,
he will dry out and be fêted,
the visitors will mark him with a kiss
and pass on.

13.
People will say of someone,
he stood outside the hut
and looked about him
and poked the ground
with a blunt stick
and looked at the clear sky
and hung his head a moment
and walked away
and never looked back.

Well, someone like him
or who could be like him,
could be mistaken for him
or might actually be him
has been seen in the market here,
if he has.

Remember the hut,
remember the ground he poked
with his blunt stick,
where he looked about him? Ah.

17.
There must have been days when alone with the cart
after the horse had died
when there was nothing much to be carried on the cart anyway
now that there were few people left to put anything on a cart
or to ride on it out and away,

when there might be a solitary book
and that found by a stranger in the mud,
when dogs barked for want of anything better to do,
when someone's name tag would be blown on to the cart,
when the cart was the only place off the ground on which to sleep.

21.
That will be enough dust for today,
we have measured and bagged enough dust.
Someone somewhere is diving into a clear, clean pool,
someone somewhere is lying laid out half asleep
on the deck of a yacht in a blue bay,
someone somewhere is eating fresh meat in a five-star hotel
discussing cricket. *Tomorrow*
we'll start early, do overtime,
get more dust measured and bagged.

23.
How many of you with kaddish sickness?
How much bread, cheese, olives?
No *malachim* seen here this year.
I know a man who says he is glad
to be dumb, again and again he tells me,
'So good to be dumb, so good.'
So it goes, putting a chair here or there
so as to change the view
from wilderness to wilderness. Kaddish sickness?
Go to a doctor, get the pills,
read the instructions, wear a mask,
play the great composers.

29.
Here is an old woman with a synagogue on her back,
it is nailed to her back,
its windows are falling out across her head,
its books are sliding out
tripping her bare feet,
her hands are making the sign of Honey Cake,
she is muttering, 'So the Most High,
blessed be His Name, has given,
so I walk.'

33.
People who never saw the synagogue will remember.
A young woman she was once now
alone in her chair, blanket over her lap,
her book laid down on the blanket. Look at her eyes.

This man carrying the lit candle through the muddy puddles,
his muttering hands, his depleted coat,
his firm faltering step. Look at his eyes.

A woman sitting in the park is told by her mother
who was told by her mother, 'In the fire
malachim appeared, benevolent, helpless.'
And, 'Your grandmother hid in the forest, in the forest.
I think she is hiding there still
and will be hiding there for ever.'

The holy place was a house of cards, someone will say,
dealt us by the Most High.
People leaning in line looked out from its balcony
with olive eyes,
the design was simple, the Torah was housed simply,
high light and deep shade fell across it evenly.

The eyes of the old couple sitting in the square,
the fire in their eyes, age was there,
its bodies heavy with the weight of the timber,
the space inside them empty where on the Sabbath they sang
Great is the Holy One and mighty is his Name,
the shriek of the space inside them now where the holy place was.

The streets will spin still in celestial space every day,
people will pass by with a map that shows no such ark,
people will pass speaking of babies and kitchen units,
of PEPs and divorces and the shortage of good cloth,
every day through the ashes, through the ashes.

35.
The Zaddik sits on the throne of numbers
for the briefest of moments

until the throne dissolves into a whisper
of what is and is not.

A cantor arrives and sings for his breakfast
thinking the night is over.

39.
Send the shadow of an angel
so that we have a holy presence
who wants to wound us
so that we can fight
the right fight
and lose
and win.

41.
And so,
if anyone asks, tell them the synagogue is closed,
soon it will be rubble tell them,
worship here now is out of the question for ever, dust
for one thing, broken floor boards for another and rot.
If anyone says they have to pray, tell them
to pray in the street or in the kitchen, well why not?
Everything is in perpetual change, tell them that,
they'll know it already, every day says it, tell them anyway,
some place, some other place, some other, other place,
say if they want to sing psalms, do it with good grace
in the bath.
                    I am
too old for this, I want a quiet life.
If anyone says they have a right,
tell them to speak to the Almighty, not to me.

Felice – Grete

A libretto

Franz Kafka, living in Prague, met at his friend Max Brod's house, in 1912, a woman called Felice Bauer. She lived in Berlin. There began a long series of letters between them, of which only Kafka's survive. At a moment when Felice had not heard from Kafka for a while, she asked her friend, Grete Bloch, to go and meet him and act as a go-between. There followed a correspondence between Kafka and Grete, alonsgide that between Kafka and Felice. Grete and Kafka met occasionally. He became formally engaged to Felice at a ceremony in Berlin, then it was broken off (at his contrivance), and the same thing happened again a few years later. Grete left some of her letters from Kafka with Felice. Hers to Kafka, aside from one draft or copy, are lost.

Felice married a businessman in Berlin and emigrated to the United States. It is thought Grete Bloch was killed in a concentration camp. All the people in this story were Jewish in a time of possible threat and upheaval, though not so much as radically to disrupt their letters or meetings or plans during those years.

It seems Kafka needed Felice and Grete as women to whom to write letters. He was ambivalent about marriage—wanted it and dreaded it.

The words here do not attempt a story, rather a sequence of the two women talking to themselves, going over and over it, in an attempt to understand what is going on, and to live with it, both in some sense in love with Kafka but not understanding what he wants, where he is in himself or in relation to them.

The friendship between Felice and Grete outlasted their relationships with Kafka, so there seems good reason to co-exist their voices, to make some of the words a dialogue—or as monologues running alongside each other duet-like, perhaps overlapping. We know nothing of conversations between them, and I haven't wanted to invent them. I have wanted to write their voices in isolation, while parallel, and co-existing in relation to the same man.

The sequence is imagined as set to music with overlaps, repeats, and not necessarily in the order as printed here.

FELICE   I must love him,
loving him's a risk,
I must love him,
he won't be loved,
I must love him,
he wants my soul,
I must love him,
he will eat me alive,
I must love him,
he won't be loved,
I must do it,
it can't be done,
I must do it,
it's not possible,
I must do it,
he won't be loved,
he will die without love,
he will eat me alive,
I must love him,
it's not possible,
I must, I must.

FELICE   I offer him myself, he turns in fright,
I offer him a home, he scorns me for it,
I say let's make it work, he tells me Kleist
to escape shot himself and was right.

I know men where I work,
I thought I knew their mind,
they settle for order's sake.

GRETE   Is his aloneness different from my own?
He writes as if from a world that is all night
to say, *Please join me, it's all right, please don't.*
I must be and I can't be can't be known.

FELICE   He can't sleep,
         he can't wake,
         he can't be,
         he can't wait,
         he is ill,
         he will fall,
         I must listen
         not question,
         must be naked
         unprotected,
         must be his,
         I must read him
         and no other,
         must be sister
         and mother,
         he wants me wholly
         and to marry
         is to die. Grete
         will be my emissary
         to make sense of him
         as a mate
         for me.

GRETE   Went between go between fell between spun,
         knew between hurt between failed between spun,
         ran between shirked between hoped between spun,
         fell spun between hurt between hurt and was spun
         and became ugly losing became forfeit.

FELICE   We could live in a nice street
         with a three-piece suite,
         be centrally-heated
         and quietly elated
         with his steady job
         and my steady job
         and children if they come
         into this stable home
         and to eat good food
         and at eleven go to bed.

FELICE   One of us would be lost and it would be me,
he knows he's lost, it has to be he says to be,
for him to be lost is his divine call
without the divine and it's hell it's hell.

He has worn me out worn me out worn me,
I have been cloth to put on take off take off,
along the track through the woods a laugh
but solemn solemn wearing me wearing me.

We walked we walked we walked we slunk,
a knife he says between us in the air—

GRETE   He says stay close and understand,
he says stay close he needs me,
he asks what's in the bleak wind,
he noticed once the day was sunny
he might have eaten me,
might have carried me,
might have taken me.
He asks what's in the bleak wind,
he says stay close and understand.

FELICE   We posed for the photograph, the camera mustn't lie,
I have it on my table here, I'd looked you in the eye,
you wrote to me you wrote to me as if you'd rather die.

I sat you stood you smiled I think you smiled it clicked.
I crossed my legs you held the chair I smiled I lacked.

You wrote to me you wrote to me as if you'd rather die,
I have it on my table here, I'd looked you in the eye,
we posed for the photograph, the camera mustn't lie.

GRETE   Not me but me but me but me but me,
you and she to be happy you and she
was the plan was the plan I agreed to, me.

Best never again never again to see me,
it was to be me not me not me not me, me,
she sent me so that you should marry her, her

her you should marry should,
my fears are well, well founded
well founded well founded well
to be bold to be bold bold bold.

The plan I agreed to the plan for you two,
for the two of you the two of you not me,
best never again never again yes not me.

FELICE   So we are heavy furniture, settle, sideboard, chest,
the dresser is what we are, four-poster, chaise,
better an empty room, he says, and an open door,
to make a home, he says, is to dig our graves.

GRETE   Another three months that's all now to survive survive
the two of you,
to survive three months more that's all surely surely
you can do that,
last three short months more and it will happen happen
that's really all.

FELICE   He wants to write to me,
not see me, not touch me,
he wants to hear from me every day
but not to see me, not to touch me,
he wants to believe I know the way,
but doesn't want to see me, doesn't want to touch me,
he has plenty to say to say to say to say.

GRETE   He knocks he knocks he knocks he hides,
he shakes my house my head my heart,
he knocks again and knocks and hides.

Wait while I catch up wait,
I've left you behind sulking,
wait while I catch up wait,
I've left you behind shaking.

He writes he writes he writes he hides,
he shakes my house my head my heart,
he writes some more and writes and hides.

Wait while I catch up wait,
I've left you behind sulking,
wait while I catch up wait,
I've left you behind shaking.

GRETE   I live in mist in mist in light in mist,
I'm everywhere a person and with him
impossible to know sensately who I am
and why and why and everywhere his frown
his frown his eyes locked
his eyes locked
his eyes locked
surgically into mine
and hers between.

FELICE   If he could go to the cemetery and laugh out loud.
If the truly dead could hear him laugh out loud,
if he could hear himself laugh privately out loud.

GRETE   He knows too much too much and more again,
he cannot live with knowing what he knows,
he knows and knows like other men are ill
with toothache or a gammy leg or piles
and is ashamed to say and has to say and says.

The mystery of the everyday,
the handling of ready money,
the incongruency of the body,

the simple smile so unruly
he has to retreat and make a note
and post it quickly from behind a gate
and wait.

GRETE   It's not his fault he was born,
it's not his fault that burden,
he didn't choose his city or his name,
his past he didn't choose his race or kin,
how tall to be how sparse how thin,
with what marked cards to play the game
after Kleist and Kierkegaard on the turn
of a harsh time, whether to walk, run,
saunter, hide, to dance, pause, burn.

FELICE   He's very smart he's never out without his coat and hat,
not any coat and hat but smart well-washed and smart,
I hope I'm up to scratch myself in the street neat, neat,
sometimes in a light suit sometimes in a dark he's smart.

GRETE   Come apart if there is apart,
at the edge of the dance a dance.
Come away if there is away,
at the edge of the dance a dance.

FELICE   This chair or that chair or this chair or that?
This door or that door or this door or that?
Step ahead step behind step ahead stop stop.

GRETE   Come apart not me not me, me,
at the edge of the dance a dance.
Come aside not me not me, me,
at the edge of the dance a dance.

FELICE   This place or that place or this place or that?
This glance or that glance or this glance or that?
Step ahead step behind step ahead stop stop.

GRETE   It hurts.

FELICE   It hurts.

GRETE   It hurts.

FELICE   It hurts.

FELICE   If he could go and stand on a bridge and scream,
just once in the middle of the night alone,
just once alone to stand right there and scream.

FELICE   He asks and he asks and he asks
and he blames,
he asks and he asks and he asks
and he shames.
It's marriage he wants,
it's marriage he fears
and it's off to the Post Office filling my ears
and my years
and my ears
and my years
with hurt.

FELICE   Keep him away from me make him come back to me.

GRETE   Make him come back to you hope he has eyes for me.

FELICE   Make some excuse for me bring him straight back to me.

GRETE   Make him come back to you oh what he writes to me.

FELICE   He wants me to say yes   to what I find monstrous,
to say yes to ugliness   when I want peace, peace.
I don't know what writing is   except in an office.
Of course I love him yes   with the formalities.
He wants me to caress   all of his writingness,
all of his writingness   all of his loneliness,
keep at a distance   and be there with kisses
in letters to kiss him   to send kisses to him.

GRETE   Friend!

FELICE   Friend!

GRETE   We have him in common.

FELICE   We have him apart.

GRETE   Who knows how to know him?

FELICE   He takes us apart.

GRETE   Friend!

FELICE   Friend!

In the wings of the bones

A week in Poland

For Cressy

I
Virginia Woolf isn't here with me
in my hotel room in Wrocław,
it's a bit late for that, nor is Bishop Colenso.
Ava Gardner isn't here with me, nor is John Keble.
They didn't travel here specially and wait.

It isn't their fault, nor Ernest Hemingway's
that he's not here,
nor Saint John the Divine's and I wish
Elizabeth Browning might have been here with me
in Wrocław in June
but they weren't to know. Only now I discover
I have failed to get this date
into their diaries.

And it would have been crowded,
even if they'd jostled for places and said, patiently,
'After you,' 'No, after you,' there'd not have been room
for all of them to sit on the bed
or on the two chairs. It would have been the
floor then or standing room only, and still waiting
to come in John Clare
and Harvey the blood circulation man
and Mr Harvey my art teacher
and a man with fruit from the Orchards of Syon
and Buster Keaton
and Mother Julian and the postman.

II
The railway tracks here at Oświęcim[1]
are not included in the Museum,
nor are the wagons,
neither the tracks nor the wagons,
neither the tracks nor the wagons

nor the streets
nor the river nor the bridge
nor the roads
nor the footprints overlaid overlaid

nor the sky, the sky here isn't listed
as a World Site. Nor are the stars,
nor this moon, surely this moon
should have a sign on it: Museum.

      I am watching
the wagons along the tracks that are not
a Museum, that are merely
wagons, tracks, that are merely wagons, tracks.
That's all they were then, it's all they are now,
wagons, tracks.

      I have curtains
cotton-thin stretched across the space between
sleep and tracks 2 to 7
between sleep and tracks 3 to 9 between 6 to 3
and 2 to 8. Through the night

front and back lights of the goods
display their light codes, goods, goods, goods
as they pass curtains
as they pass curtains these curtains. The trick
curtains have curtains have curtains
have is what curtains have.

      But listen, the Hassidim
are in a trance
of dance in a cattle truck. What is it with loud wings

will come rushing out of the sky to lead the procession
out of this canopy? Will float away
the mothers with their children,
will fly the old and the sick clandestinely towards
a family table?

In the new station café
cased in walls aside from the tracks,
in the station café
aside a cry's length from the tracks,
in the station café
I have spilt my glass of *habata*[2] and it
makes an uneven pool
on the wooden table. The saucer is in the pool
but not floating on it.
I have righted the glass on the saucer
but very little tea is left.
The woman is smiling
as I say *Sorry*, again *Sorry*,
in a translatable tone of voice
as she wipes the table
and takes it all away, *Sorry*,
Lipton's tea bag, plastic spoon,
saucer, glass with the mouthful of *habata* in it,
soggy serviette, while outside
the trucks rattle past, the trucks rattle past

and the clock here will be a cripple always,
no matter how many clean trains
pass through as *per* the timetable,
however many good jokes are told
and homely anecdotes related up line and
down line in the tense present of the
blue-white carriages   the clock
ticks on crutches,
its hands
rip apart minutes and glue them together again
so that everything appears to be
as *per* the timetable in its innermost
spring-locked-texture-of-jelly-babies

tongue-clotted orderly
locked jaw set-piece — From platform No. 1

I watch a little passenger train on the
very early morning run
between loganberries and clocking in.

It's a dinky little train, quiet, smooth-running,
running-ordinary along these tracks
in the very early morning summer light. No poem

      can keep track of these trains,
here's another now, more trucks, head down, eyes front.

III
Buttercups in Auschwitz
and heather
and daisies
and dandelions
and these tiny, fragile, pretty trefoils
are doing very well
and the grass is nicely fresh green
and there are forget-me-nots
and fine healthy poplars higher
  than the brick barracks,

and there is Lipton's in a glass
with lemon or milk
and lumps of white sugar

and good food, too,
with a menu in
Polish, German, Hebrew and English

and it costs nothing to get into the camp
and the sun is shining
and where it says *Halt!*
we don't have to. And I have seen a report of

a man who says
'if there'd been grass
I'd have eaten it.'

              So have I come here to
interview the bones, to interview
the dust in the pond, have I come here
to interview shivers of smoke?
They seem not to make good interviewees
but still
I have my notebook ready.

  The Hassid dancing in his own small yard,
  is a Hassid for torture and gas and fire,
  and if not the Hassid then his wife and children.
  The Hassid's dance is to be burned right out.

Is there someone present here with a friend?
Is there someone in line who remembers a friend?
Which of you dying misses a friend?
Is there someone here who would like to name a friend?
Before you fall and get the bayonet in your eye
is there someone here who would like a new friend?

A name on a wall, a prayer made to a wall.

      This Mordecai,
        this Mordecai here
in the bunks when he dribbles out a cry says
one of us in this freezing hut
has in his soul the light that can light other souls
and I whisper like a torn rag, please, please, who is
that man, is it Leo?
            Mordecai—well we know him,
we know Mordecai—he tries now to
unfold, to unfold a hand, I'm sure
he has a hunch—am I right Mordecai, a hunch?
Is it Josef whose head is always turned a little
askantwise? I would say he nods his head if this
sagging from his neck is not now always—

Who ever believed it anyway? I try to close my eyes.
Who ever thought one of us was—so all of us were—
chosen with light? Back then, oh yes,
but now, now? Whoever it is—Mord, is it Nathan?
We need that light, all of us. Who is it?

What does crazy Mordecai know anyway?
He was a purveyor of nonsense even before—
we all know it, we all are going gaga with hunger.
Who is it, then, Mordecai?
Point your wobbly finger, do it, man, put the splint
of a man's name in my ear, name him, is it Janos who
folds himself in but is always looking? Who then?—
point or name him and I shall grab the hem
where his shawl would have been—Who
from this unbridgeable distance—

They've all gone—
grave unbound,
stone-less—to ashes and
the thing about this tiny piece of sharp brick
is that it has a slice of broken toe in it,
it has clog marks,
and it is red, red. This piece of rubble, brick rubble.
Underfoot brick rubble.
Brick rubble witness.
Yes, I can see broken toe pressed into it
and clog marks, I know
why it is red, I can see red, red,
torn feet, to the bone.
                    Look again, the brick is clean,
only the brick itself is broken.
The sun is soul-bright through the hut window,
the door is open.

                    At the cross-section of the decision
here in all weathers
in the photo taken by the SS Officer
after the arrival of a long train of trucks. Let's call
the elderly woman with the headscarf Ruth
and let's call the taller woman behind her
with the full hair Naomi. Here is, let's say, Carmel
with her baby Isaac in her arms walking (directed?) away.
Here, their backs to us, are Adina and Leah, let's say,
and between them
holding their hands is little Ellie, let's say. There is
such a crowd of them, all named, all known. Who are
these men in stripes looking on as the SS uniforms—
Karl, let's say, and Peter—
do the directing? They seem only casually engaged,
this Eli and Jacob and Franz, let's say.

Waiting around they would all
have heard *You, You, You*, that's all, that's all, *this way,
faster, more faster—You, You, You.*
Look, there, deep in the crowd, is Abigail, let's say,
hand in hand with her daughter, Sarah. Here
where we stand now.

           There isn't a photo but
work done and food longed for
here comes Karel[3] flip-flopping
in his odd boots, the vocation golden,
the predictions ancient,
the memory sorrowful, the eyes soft.

I never tried to hide, hiding was impossible.
A single curlew flew in looking for crumbs,
there were no crumbs, Louis sang Jonah
aloud under his breath, Felix cried without tears,
Tomas rambled to himself loudly and was shot.

It's like a horse trying to make a fire,
trying to make a fire on which to create eggs.

Jacko was lonely and pulled faces,
we were all lonely and pulled faces,
Jacko's faces made us forget our own.
I see Jacko's face still in the mirror, like rain.

It's like an elm trying to sprout daisies,
trying to sprout daisies to give in the darkness
to The One Whose Name Must Not Be Spoken.

Claudio's neck was a running sore
as if Abraham's knife was nesting there.
Jacko and Ezra together sucked it out,
gave praise all three that they had a neck at all.

It's like a doughnut trying to be best pork,
trying to be pork to celebrate the Sabbath.

We did our best when we knew what best was.
When we failed we prayed to the Most High
to turn away an eye, if possible two,
but not to close The Heart, not to close The Heart.

Karel clanks away in his odd boots,
the vocation golden, the predictions ancient,

the memory sorrowful, escape funny,
the having been here terrible, for ever.

School groups
are being shown round knowing
each other's and the teachers' names where

numbers in numbers by numbers
stood
for hours upon hours in extreme cold
on the parade ground
here where the casual bullet
and the multiple gallows
and the *death wall*—

I have knelt
in one gas chamber
and at the ruins of another.
I whisper trying to
know what I am saying this is a holy place

outside of the niceties,

a rejection museum to be kept open. I have seen
the heaps of women's hair
and the children's shoes
and the grown-ups' shoes

and the spectacles and the suitcases with names
and the prayer shawls. There is

such nonsense here
only saying nothing will do, so much

nothing I struggle to say it
where only *holy* will do, only *holy*,
its impatience flagrant.

Nothing, then. But still
a small breeze here needs an amanuensis already?

There isn't a Suggestion Box
and a little slip of paper and a stub of pencil
for saying what we think
might be for the best,
then to pop it in.
                    There is no
    checklist with tick boxes:
    Work is Freedom □ □ □ □
    The orchestra was a great idea □ □ □ □
    etcetera.
                    No one
gives us a sheet asking
  Have you enjoyed your hiatus?
  Will you again be visiting us?
  Will you be recommending us to a friend?

There isn't a reminder: *Please make sure
you take all your personal belongings—*
etcetera.

The Museum doesn't have a star rating.

  How hard was the bed?
  How effective the kick?
  How sweet the gas?

IV
In the pantomime of sleep soup of the day let's say
courgette mozzarella bangles of
primary colours with a little turquoise a dousing
of argument name wall light drop one clap
for awakening two for mime is a pretty coverlet three
is a wall of shoes how to wipe a
poem free of dust four wheel of rules is
pretty coverlet for eye-draught no time to
waste sing a growling noise five is heavy train dear
rhetoric dear dark
dear wide entrance six into *you know how it is*
the hole in the wall the coloured rain seven a wall
in the mouth stack of hair eight into acclaim oil of
gathered to raise itself initiation pretty coverlet
stranger face to face nine flower-field in the
throat last week hit the envelope
of air where the long grass where
the river the stitchwort ten the suitcases.

Someone says there is no time to waste so sing,
there is a growling noise heavy rain
                on stone.

        Judenfleck[4]
on the window of the sleeve,
still/life dissolves into fancy dress drizzle,
a fish swims into a blanket and stays there
wearing *Judenfleck* like salt and pepper.
Open the prayer book at the blank page,
fail to disappear into its name, *Judenfleck*.

Through the trees one a growling noise stack
of hair to have shared a truck breeze
in your eyes my friend two broken on a head down
dumb allowance to be parsed to keep up three
hill of shoes pigeon low-flying breeze in your eyes in
four your throat a world's length story scrolls
home discomfort song
for return five this mendicant while on show

lining up each suitcase carefully inscribed six a
reign of dust flagration of alert here's another now
breeze off the water tickle seven to
have not cried together eight in hock the
note the customary
tremble quick now nine the law
to find its home in us where the river the stitchwort
bread the throat causing ten such and such.

Someone says there is no rain to waste so growl,
there is a singing noise heavy time on stone.

Long drift of scent of skin without a map.

Standing with his moustache by the piano
he likes to think he is her zealous windmill,
fire of itself doesn't want *Judenfleck*, Mrs,
bones come running with an empty bowl,
this face has too many eyes, catch the tail
of a cockerell, go for a finger tip flute-flight.

You know the breeze I mean, the dumb burden.

Towards a side door look breeze off the water.

If I can hold you firmly by the hand
and spin you round and round
I can send you spinning high above the clouds
out of harm's way.

V
As we drive on to Crakow we are still
where we were and
deep in the throat of my guts I am so angry
it could burn me up, anger
has its claws in me, a faultline
is ready to break open,
to split me apart from myself. But

there is no one to be angry with. My tongue
is a boat whose rudder-Amen
is swinging loose. The skull-cap I wore

in the newly recreated synagogue
where there is no longer a congregation
   —*Happy are those who live in your house*[5]
   —*Establish abundant peace on your people*
   —*Shalom*
                in
Oshpitzin / Oświęcim / Auschwitz

is the roof of the cabin of the boat
whose rudder-Amen
is swinging loose in the pond
where the ashes are.

                Now
in the Tempel Synagogue we sit at prayer desks
for where the rhythm of knowledge—

For the flirtatious flutter with the Most High
in the rhythm of knowledge and supplication—

Preserve us at our prayers up and down up and down
            at our prayers preserve us
         from the stage fright of the end.

   5 zlotis to get in, a small heap of skull caps
      to be worn (I wear one), no postcards, and

in the Old Jewish cemetery
it is raining real rain
like in England, but on Hebrew here, and now

we are eating in the vegetarian restaurant
on *ul. Gertrudy* along from where St Stanislaus
in his silver coffin these hundreds of years
is high perched in the cathedral
in the castle

where in the great arched courtyard of the king
I doubt any Hassid ever danced
where the red ants are.

Names on stones in the cemetery may not be
who is under them. Stones hidden or broken were
put back by the remnant and we are

drinking tea in the vegetarian restaurant
then eating a good mid-day meal: cabbage and mushroom
in dumplings, fried potato pancakes with sauce
and now a coffee.

Some names in this city drew gassing and burning,
a disappearing trick was tried against a whole people.

A young man has arrived quietly at the next table,
he has a cup of tea, he leans back in his chair, is quiet,
is reading Rimbaud.

The chairs here are like tombstones, for an hour
—less than an hour—our names are on them.
We have our passports and soon will return home.

Over the tannoi Rameau and Beethoven have been
followed by the Hallelujah Chorus. On the turn at
'He shall reign for ever and ever' a tram now, then,
rattles past the window.

The Gestapo
did well by its own darkness,
no Hassidim now in Poland, hardly a Jew at all,
no great congregations,
no dance continuing on through the generations.
A few old books, yes,
and a few synagogues restored. Here in Crakow
the Old Synagogue is a museum. Look,
   in one corner great leather-bound books,
      fifteen of them, used, a candle
         that could be lit, a kettle
      that could boil water if asked,
         shawls that were worn.

VI
Off-stage around a corner. This corner?
A secret, for ever.

    Little blue umbrella
    coming in a barrow
    pushed by a kind fella.

What we call a *moment*,
to name a *reverie*
that passed quickly.

I can't see, never will see,
so long as—

    In the wings of the bones
    there's a secret travel agent
    with whom one always wins.

Can't hear the sea from here,
the tidal Whose Name—

    Swimming back stroke
    very slowly
    on the bloody ground wake.

If this line were to go this way
or some other—Speaking of other—
If a tired curling finger—

VII
Never day by day, it seems, are the churches
of Crakow vacant, and on Sundays packed
to the pavement, these huge temples.

On the night tide here in Częstochowa
they petition the Holy Mother
Queen of Heaven bejewelled Matron,
Black Madonna, a painting, a Saviour.

A woman has left her bag in the middle
of the crowding chapel floor. Now—
we don't know why—she returns and has
moved it a little and moved herself

away and again
a while later she revisits and moves it,
where again people newly arriving
walk around the bag, stand

alongside the bag while the prayers
continue busily beyond the rood
at the altar where never smiling Mary—

We eat in the monastery café—a block-hut
in the car park—and return to the chapel
of the Black Madonna, to the prosthetics
left behind as evidence, to the buzz of attention.

But for my swollen, infected painful toe
we find along the wide avenue a pharmacy,
where in English I display my naked foot

and am sold a packet of ointment plus a few
bandages and by the next day my toe
is more like its normal size and not hurting.

John Paul II was here in Częstochowa
three times. Maybe
he had a swollen toe and
didn't know there was a pharmacy.

VIII
In the large White Stork Synagogue not long since
handed back to the few Jews of Wrocław
and renovated plainly as far as cash raised so far
will allow

> three musicians and a singer
> perform for a TV crew

and I try to write a poem:

> 'Sing to the walls the old songs,
> sing to the plastic chairs,
> sing to the upper levels lacking plaster,
> sing to the light through the dome windows,
> sing to the floor once well trodden,
> sing to the echo the old songs,'

etcetera.
> No
booklet history, no postcards,
no service books. There was a box of
cardboard skull-caps
and I wear one. Perhaps

only because of the TV crew
are we able to get in.
> Then it is

back to the airport where there are men in camo
to whom I declare
my coat with my camera in it and my pens,
and I declare my belt (and have to take it off)
and my watch (and have to take it off)
and my wallet with its metal clasp—
it all goes into the plastic tray—for inspection.
Just as well I have no gold fillings in my teeth
nor a gold ring. But it's OK, these big uniformed blokes
short of words and we short of theirs are newly
EU men.

Now

fasten your prayers,
read the emergency notation,
be a fledgling cantor in a bowl of cloud,
declare with tears the minor key,
dream the dream of the escapologist
impatient for the home tune.

Sunny up here
with our names intact,
look, spare burial space, spare

soul space and I'd like to
ask the Baal Shem[6] what he knew about flying.
Perhaps he is a transmigrated soul
here on the aeroplane
above the clouds—and what clouds today!—
here awake, eyes closed, in an ecstasy
of weeping or
in his shawl waiting alert and bent invisible to me,
for when we all will be caught up
without benefit of metal, kerosene,
passport or charm.

IX

Without glow,[7] mere pretence of sight only,
only gap, split-eye, blossom of lucid scar,
only hole, pit, piteous lake only,
time-spent inscription lacking conclusive reach,
I give you hiatus, blank, the want of clue only,
slippery hollow, fluid and curious, sung waste,
the display cavernous, never to be recompensed
as sense, the field puckered, mere whisper only
of connective tissue, mouth gone.

X
I bring home my little sac of electrified wire
sparking blue cold-purple bruise.
I bring it as a fragile souvenir,
I bring it as it was wound around me,
I want to find it a good home here,
my little bag of sparking electrified wire.

When I wake my arms ache
with the weight
of my little sac of electrified wire. I read,

'There is another place where women can be found:
No. 10, the experimental block. The women in No. 10
are being artificially inseminated, injected
with typhoid and malaria germs, or operated on.
The women are kept behind barred and
boarded-up windows—'[8]
        and from my armchair I reach across
to the pack of my prints I had today from Jessop's,
and here it is, No. 10. And here is a photo of me
sitting on the steps of the block opposite,
resting after all that walking.

It was too easy as well
to *take a photo* in the gas chamber,
then one of the oven. I knew it. Still I did it.

XI
I slip into poem-speech
even as I am ignorant all over again
of what poem-speech is, how it works.
what use it is.

Aside I say my toes hurt,
one toe especially, I say
my arthritic leg hurts, I say it is
time again to put the kettle on,
I say I am too tired to write.

I am moved by a few words
of someone else's poem—
so this is it, this is why—
but what is a tear or two, a wrench,
a tickle, a thought, a heartache
in my room alone?

I am a tourist.
Even in my own street now,
in my own heart now
I shall be a tourist.

I think there is something to be won.
As has been said of goodness,
                    of love,
regardless of pain. It has been said
fire burns
and frees. I write this.

XII

The thing is, there is a secret,
the way a crab begins to crawl up a wall
then pauses and climbs back down.
Or it's the turn in the weather
the way a good conversation perceives it.
Or a long distance train pulls in
and the driver calls out, *Hey, you, there's—*
what did I do with it? The message,
I've lost it. Or on the way to the end of comfort,
there is a look from one face to another.
Or a finger touching, also without words.

And here she comes the provisional *habata* lady
with pieces of a glass on a tray nicely.
She says she is not thinking straight,
can't stand up beyond the curve of song, she says,
and indicates her weight of thought.
She says she is trying to decipher on the freezer
a word that may be *ingredients* but may
equally be something else—she squints at me—
more sour
to do with waiting on the breezy quay
for that purring boat, she says, you know, Sir.
I do a little skip and a hop without standing up.
She brings me
the head of a catfish on a flowered saucer
and curtsies, and before I can thank her
a few minutes later returns with sugar
and throws it at me. We are getting there so I
ease myself in. Lovely *cuppa-habata*, she says,
when she brings the outboard motor.
I sigh towards the notional horizon and say,
allow me, and together we heave it against
its better knowledge
on to the tablecloth. We position it fit
for the journey that must be taken elastically.
I believe I have caused this calamity,
she thinks she has brought me *habata*.
Clearly she is at heart an excellent *habata* lady
if only I was able to ask adequately.

NOTES

1 Three names refer to the same town: Oświęcim (Polish), Oshpitizin (Yiddish), Auschwitz (German).

2 'habata' (as I spoke it)—'tea'

3 'Here comes Karel now' owes a debt of story and weight to an account by Primo Levi.

4 Judenfleck: the Star of David that Jews were obliged to wear.

5 'Happy are those . . .' A website tells me these words were spoken at the reopening of the Oświęcim synagogue Jewish Centre.

6 The Baal Shem Tov lived during the second half of the 18th century in south-east Poland. He was founder of the Jewish movement, Hassidism.

7 'Without glow . . .' was prompted by an OED email 'word of the day'.

8 'There is another place . . .' is quoted from *This way to the gas, ladies and gentlemen*, prose memory stories by the Polish writer, Tadeusz Borowski.

Towards the line

—five—

Here comes a man

Here comes a man carrying my bones on a cushion.
He whispers to someone around a corner
that the map is missing, stolen, he says, as like as not.

I say, I never did learn to play the spinnet,
so what does it matter? I think there is to be a ceremony,
my bones are to be deposited in a demolished hut.

He whispers it again, as like as not, and again,
he is loving every minute of saying it, *as like as not*,
as my bones are moved on by this procession of one,

and someone is rebuilding the demolished hut
but lazily, without conviction, being promised pay
that will never come. My bones are rocking on the cushion

because the man carrying them is getting high on
as like as not, as like as not, while the hut
is neither one thing nor the other. What was a shelf

is floating away on the winded sand. My hut-idea
is a canary-cage coming along behind carried with
nonchalance by a man in a cloak so too big

for him he keeps tripping over it and my hut-idea sways
and hits the ground almost. Perhaps retreat
is what we do when there isn't a sign or when there

is a sign but what it means has been forgotten.
On the edge of the desert now everyone comes to a
strict stop. As if they have forgotten their purpose.

There are no chairs

For Charles Johnson

There are no chairs flying past the window here today.
I shall describe them: office swivels with red seats,
leather-covered easy chairs, waiting room chairs in threes,
none of these is flying past the window today, none of them.
No plain dining chairs either, no chairs with book-rests,
no chairs from Norway or Luxemburg, nor from Spain.
No collisions of chairs out there today, I'm glad to say,
nothing broken in flight, no apologies necessary.
No chairs arm in arm either, which is sad, no pushy chairs,
no bright green plush chairs, no deckchairs folded or in a flap.
I have of course sat here ready, alert, staying awake,
and the window is so wide, so clear, with so much sky.

Large darkness

I made my first large darkness in a back lane in Highgate,
inviting likeness I scuffed and blemished it,
it was the smudge of a likeness in delegated space,
with a reckless voice, apprenticed there,
by being almost absent almost present to be calling me.

The second darkness was not long in coming.
I was in Blackheath exactly on long walks backwards
and forwards and sideways my arms hung loose
with no reach, design was bleak in me at crossed purpose,
the darkness was there all day inviting me, close to, blessing hurt,
I had no choice but to make it, entitling it *Darkness 2*
to leave it behind, having outflown it.

Darkness 3, though, was making its cold demands on me
across the brook-brook, more subtle than *Darkness 2*, God
who at devious times and in subtle places, the pain inarticulate,
the grief palimpcestuous, immodesty overtook me
and I made the third darkness, in stark, bright colours.

Allowing for no fourth or further darkness, thinking no fourth
or beyond had been envisaged by the Maker in me conceptually
to lurch me, the soft tissue began to be clawed more fiercely
like a cat with a sparrow, soon wingless with only a voice
strangled out of the invisible wound,—
                              And so it was, looking like a person,

on a Tuesday on my way to the coast and beyond, in a field,
I woke, an irreparable traveller, longing still to sing,
trying to give voice to even a faint *Yes,* and *Darkness 4,* larger, darker
might have been made. It eluded me, appearances
notwithstanding, I protest, I was without walls, but yes,
astray, put beyond reach, without solace, all stillness broken,
vacated to poetry, this, this.

Of the colours

For Judy, Peter, Rosie and Nicola at the Wast Hills

It is enough to be here.

It is enough to be here.

It is enough to be here
but what if tomorrow
there has been a poem

of the young cows nosing towards us,
closer and around us and closer still,
until we moved?

What if next week, next year
there has been a poem
that says a duck splattered the bullrushes
and flew off over the hawthorn in flower?

It is enough to be here on this hot day's evening,
but what if there is a poem of the sun going down
over the sound of a far motor bike,
a poem that remembers the farm in the valley
so near to the city boundary?

What if there is a poem
of the long shadows, of the colours we wore:
red, purple, yellow, grey, a black coat
in the long sloping green
where the sheep are,
towards the Malverns, the Abberleys, the Lickeys,
us sitting on blankets with the remains of our picnic
or walking here and there,
our shadows outgrowing us, knowing, cooler now,
we'd be home before dark.

I lay my head on the ground
as if in the open tent many years ago, letting the world go by.
I like it, I like the feel of it, us, the smell of the grass.

Fine line

The church wasn't open
so I sat outside with the dead people
and their flowers.

None of the dead people rose up to meet me,
I was too early for the big day,
there were no trumpets.

I told them I ache for love.
How neat, bright and cute the flowers are,
a breeze moves them but not much,
they will see out their sentry duty
then fade away quietly.

I am so tired I wonder at the fine line
between me and the dead people.
They don't make poems.
They are not thirsty.
I want to lie down, but not alone,
nor yet for ever.

Part of a day
Whitby, December 04, for Myra Connell

Lost 6p on a roll-a-2p coin machine,
took photos of lobster pots,
looked up the 191 steps to the abbey,
had a pot of tea in the station café,
bought by mistake a blackcurrent and apple pie,
spent 20p in the civic loo,
went on the Endeavour, turned away from
the man demonstrating a seaman having his leg cut off
and his stump stuck in boiling tar,
spent 20p again in the civic loo,
sat on the quay and watched people pass
and beyond them boats gliding in with purpose,
bought, in a back street, sheep wool soap and
secondhand poems by Yehuda Amichai and by
Michael Donaghy, both gone now.

Dixit Dominus

For Rebecca Farmer

Here's a man on the radio talking about Vivaldi's Dixit Dominus,
and here it is now, Dixit Dominus, a fast coach ride through a
bracing wind across what once was heath, now my kitchen.
Here's a postcard from the Jewish cemetery in Prague,
and look at me in my red dressing gown after midnight.

A ship has come in bringing people home from destruction,
not much to say except it's good to be back on solid home ground,
and Dixit Dominus is jogging now, now pausing at a trough,
the Jewish cemetery in Prague is sepia,
my dressing gown is made from synthetic velvet,
it's good that my friend in Orpington has mended her drains.

Perhaps something buried in the garden is worth mentioning:
it looks like a blade with an agate handle, or it's a dead fish.
Dixit Dominus will come and go, trotting now, now into a gallop.
Tombs inscribed in Hebrew, bunched up, they lean.
I'd like to wear my dressing gown in the street but I won't.
Dixit Dominus has stopped, the man is talking again. What next?

When she asked

When she asked if the world had ended yet
a bird flew from her blue hands and out
through the ward's closed window.

She asked then if I'd take her out to tea
to the park where the limes are, to the café,
and I lied and said there was rain forecast.

She whispered, *Come closer,* and took my hand,
she asked me softly if the world had ended yet.
A forest grew up around us and it was night.

When her eyes closed on the floating pillow
a procession of lions filed past the window
all of them winking woefully a red eye.

Her lips were playing, *Has the world ended yet?*
I touched her arm and ants rushed out,
making a trail of themselves towards the door.

When her finger drew tiny circles on the sheet
a child came out from under the bed
with a voice so open with song I was startled

and thought I would fall and be for ever lost.
And when I looked again the bed was empty
and I went begging them, for a crust, a crust.

This is the singer

This is the singer we picked up in the café in the hills,
he said he is no longer a singer but we think he is,
he has the slant gaze of it and offered always a long pause
before replying to any question, then changed key
with his eyes. He was shy when we met him and he is
more shy now. He stopped speaking at all
three days ago and conveys now only pause and
no longer smiles or
conveys
any emotion whatsoever, not even
when nibbling at the scrambled egg we try to offer him
whenever we can steal eggs because he seemed at first
to relish it. But look at him,
isn't it a singer you see standing here, one of the best?
Isn't he alone with himself the way a singer is?
We think perhaps he will sing plaintively for you if you
give him a hard, narrow bed and a view of the sea.
We will leave you our best camera and his shoes.

Still here

Still here the hut at the edge of the desert
where if I could find myself now I am here still.

Inside the hut there's coffee in its jar
and a box of good tea
and there's fresh milk
and a tin of biscuits.

The single tree is here. Someone is waiting still
behind the tree. Something must happen now.
Or not.

Nine Songs

Versions of the 3rd century BCE Chinese

1. THE GREAT ONE SPIRIT

'It's a lucky day, there are good signs,
 give reverence that will please the Great One Spirit.'

2. TO THE MOUNTAIN CLOUD SPIRIT

I have washed in spring water sweetly scented.
My clothes lighten, I am as beautiful as Trefoil,
as becoming as Forget-me-not.

   'Look, swirling around the Clent Hills,
   look, the Spirit is coming down to us,
   in a blaze of brightness, look now!'

Our holy place is simple but built with our best skills,
built with the finest materials we could find,
but for such a Spirit it is hardly more than a hut.
But here he comes, between sun and moon
riding in his dragon chariot, hovering close,
coming now even closer, now swirling away,
now coming again closer,—

   'You can see the Clent summit through the mist,
   the mist clears, you can see the clouds over the hill,
   that's where the Mountain Cloud Spirit hides.'

I have ached to dance, and at last you are here—
Smell the fresh grass and the sweat of the dancers!

   'Be the sound now, my friends, and the sounding board!'

So soon and you are away,
up and turned away faster than I can catch you.
I can never hold you, all I can catch is my own breath,
I catch the shout in my own breath
and it nearly chokes me, you are away, away.

The Mountain Cloud Spirit looks back at us,
over the Clee Hills he goes, over the Cambrian Mountains,
soon he will be over every place known.

I sigh a sigh of great longing, I am sad, sad, heart-broken.

3. THE ELUSIVE WOMAN OF THE SEVERN

The Elusive Woman of the Severn hasn't come,
she is taking her time, she'll give me a heart attack.
On the island in mid-stream she is waiting for someone.
I shall change into my best clothes and out in my rowing boat
I shall find her, so long as the Severn
and the Plinlimmon Hills stay calm.

There she is! But she is not coming to me.
She is playing her boran, but who for?

    'Drum with the sticks now!
    Drum with the stones to greet her!
    Make a great racket!'

Now driving her winged dragons she goes north.
I turn my boat towards where the river divides
and I row as fast as I can upstream. My disguise
is Teasel and Hogweed bound with Bindweed,
my paddles are made of willow, the bunting
that waves from my boat is Willow Herb and Charlock:
isn't this enough?! I stare and stare across the furthest
furthest stretch of the river and she is there.

    'What are throats for? What are tongues for?
    Breathe out the persuade-song!'

She is there astride the great Severn,
she raises herself higher and higher, higher and higher,
her attendants follow her, take up my deep cry.
With me they let out a great sigh, and my tears
are blown away
in endless spray.

        'Drum with the sticks!
        Drum with the stones!
        Make a deafening racket!'

My longing
for the Elusive Woman is deep and terrible,
my willow oars merely chip the ice,
my steering pole of weathered ash merely whisks the snow.
Could anybody pick hazel nuts from the water?
Could anyone gather water lilies from the poplar tree?

When two hearts have not been brought together
what can a match-maker do but despair? A pledge
not even given the eye can be said to have been broken.

These rocky shallows are hard to paddle through.
Even as I struggle, the flying dragons are taking her far away.
All I've known of this love is grief, and the grief is deeper now
than ever. Didn't we have an agreement ? Didn't she break it?

   'Good people, the shaman is tired,
   all day he has danced,
   all day he has watched and waited.'

At dawn I galloped my horses through the lowlands
                to the river,
now in the evening I keep to myself at the river's
                eastern shore,
the birds settle on the roof tops, the waters circle
around the meeting hall and I drop my silver ring into the river,
it was my wedding gift.
                'Let her go now,
let the Elusive Woman of the Severn go,
we will come together another day,
we'll come together another bright day.'

On this fragrant bank where she was I pick Speedwell
in case there's a chance to give it to one of her attendants,
but I know the moment has passed
and here I am still, pacing up and down, hanging around.

4. STILL WAITING FOR THE ELUSIVE WOMAN OF THE SEVERN

I am sure she will come today to the eastern bank.
The daughter of the Great Spirit of Plinlimmon
will certainly come today to the eastern shore.

    'Fill the circle, good people, with an expectant silence,
      the drums will be properly heard then, so will the flutes,
      so will your songs and your great shouts.'

Your eyes, my love, are looking somewhere else far away,
in my boat I feel desolate with sadness.

The autumn wind starting up makes waves on the river,
the autumn wind for fun brings down leaves from the trees.

    'Our shaman is hurt, he is hurt and still must fly,
      our shaman must borrow the wings of the heron,
      our shaman must borrow the feathers of the hawk,
      our shaman must borrow the heart of the raven.'

Hurl me into the sky, my friends! Hurl me high
with your strong voices! With your shaking arms
send me on the flying journey.

We made an agreement to meet this evening, didn't we?
Look, I am standing tall straining my eyes across the kale.
Would an eagle roost in the duck-weed?
Would a fish-net be useful at the top of a tree?

    'Offer the White Campion, offer the Toadflax,
      offer the Knapweed. Let these flowers
      sing to the Elusive Woman of the Severn.'

The Avon has its swans, the Rea has its tiny rapids,
I long for you, woman, I dare not speak and I have to speak,
I can't stop speaking, everything is blurred as I try to see,
I can see only the waters swirling close to me.
Would a bull sing in the market?

Would the salmon be out on the bank? This morning I
sprinted like crazy across the lowlands by the great river,
because I'd heard she had asked to see me.

'All of you, dance more! You have danced all day
but keep dancing, you have shouted,
you have thrown yourselves to the ground
and grown up again like the great forest,
you have turned your bodies as the day has turned,
you have exhausted yourselves in an ecstasy of seeking,
and now keep dancing!'
Surely
the Shadowy Spirits can't be coming already
as many as the clouds
down from the Plinlimmon Hills to fetch her back!

'Shake the cones, my friends,
give them a good rattle!'

I throw my ring into the flooding river,
I leave my watch on the bank,
in a backwater I run and find Bilberries,
they will be a gift to the woman I love.
I know the moment has passed but even so,
walking up and down I wait and I wait.

5. THE GREAT FESTIVAL OF THE SPIRIT OF LIVING AND DYING

The gates of heaven are open! On a dark cloud
I am riding off in that direction, winds give me speed!
Showers of rain keep the dust down!

'The Spirit of Living and Dying, my friends,
sweeps the sky today and is coming towards us.
Our shaman will leave far below the earth that lifes us,
she will attend the Great Spirit, impatiently we will
wait to hear the story of our living and dying.'

I am coming towards you flying on pure air,
you are the Great Spirit, I am the humble lover,
yet together we will travel over the Malverns,
over the Black Mountains and the Preseli Mountains.

    'Her spirit-cloak trails as she flies higher,
      her strings of beads trail loose, you understand,
      my friends, the fearful crisis, our lives in the balance.'

I am alone in the clouds, my love, where are you?
Didn't I pick lovely ripe blackberries for you? Didn't I?

    'The Great Spirit of Living and Dying
      has driven his dragon chariot
      thundering, O my dear friends, back into Heaven.'

Age bends me lower and lower.
Not to draw nearer is to drift further apart.
After all that had seemed promised, here I am sitting alone
making daisy chains. Shit! For what ?!

6. THE FESTIVAL OF THE HEALER OF LIVING
AND DYING

Now in autumn the brambles and the heather grow thick
around our meeting place.
                          I feel dizzy from the perfume
of the memory of juicy green, of white flowers dazzling.

    'The wild thyme sharpens our shaman's longing
      and the memory of the healer of living and dying
      fills the place with beauty.'
                        The Healer of Living and Dying
picks me out. He comes saying nothing,
          only I know he is present, and he goes away again
saying nothing. He rides off in the whirlwind,
          the clouds are his banners, but he knows I am here.

    'Be patient, my friends, our shaman is tired,
      the Great Healer of Living and Dying also is resting,

but be patient.'

                 No sorrow is worse than this parting,
for no joy is greater than such a meeting.
               In a coat of Rhododendron tied with Basil
I was prepared here, and suddenly he came,
               and as suddenly he has gone.

    'The Healer of Living and Dying expects of us patience.'

I bathed with you in the Pool of Heaven,
you dried my hair on the Hill of Sunshine.

    'The Healer of Living and Dying is far away now
    in his chariot, but he has not forgotten us,
    our shaman will be ready in her seagull feathers,
    we will fly our heron banners.'

I have waited for you but you do not come,
I have shouted into the wind my wild song.

7. TO THE BRIGHT SPIRIT OF THE WEST

The sky begins to light up, soon he will wake, a little light
shivers the waking of the rowan tree on to my balcony.
I feel my body to remind myself what kind of thing I am,
I close my eyes and try to remind myself what thing I am,
night becomes pale and in the full light I open myself.

    'In your spirits climb the hill, in your bone souls climb,
    in your song-bones climb, climb to support our shaman,
    breathe bright to support our shaman's flight.'

His harnessed chariot has the sign of the dragon,
the wheels are thunder-driven, trail clouds twist and turn,
he lets out a great sigh and looks back, full of desire,
then looks down, singing,
               What a beautiful woman!
And how beautiful the music!   But if I linger I shall forget
what it is to be a Bright Spirit.   The flutes are brightening.

one drum speaks to another,   the bells are being beaten
till the bell-stands rock, I am caught   by flutes, by cymbals,
the astute, beautiful woman   comes towards me like a swan,
she knows verse-play, O yes!   with measured abandon!

> 'My friends, many spirits have heard our music
>   and are coming, darkening the sun.'

In his coat of blue cloud   and in his rainbow cloak
he is grasping the reins,   the chariot is hauled away,
he is going to leave me.   Oh but I'm taken up with him,
I am high in the clouds with my love.   He speaks a spell
against the Wolf of Heaven   and from the Great Cup
offers me a drink of Heaven's   sweet wine.

Swallowing our shaman's thoughts the Bright Spirit
will plunge into the dark pit and be lost and powerless
until turned again, by the moon.

8. TO THE OLD RIVER GOD

I have flirted with you in your nine tributaries.
A whirlwind came and whipped up your waters
into fierce waves, I rode your waves in my boat:
its prow is your own dragon, its vestments are
White Dead Nettle, its banner is the reflection
           of your water serpent,
the song of the journey I have rehearsed all winter.

> 'Strike the tuned gongs, let the tuned gongs sing out,
>   let the drums speak, send the message of the drums
>   to the Old River God.'
>   *I have climbed Carn Ingli*
> *and I have seen all the meanderings of Afon Gwaun,*
> *of your secret journey to the great ocean,*
> *my heart cut, my whole body ploughed up, distraught.*

> 'You are the Gwaun, you are the flow of the Gwaun,
>   you are the *cwm* through which the Gwaun flows.
>   Flow to the sea then, my friends, let the flow through.'

Night almost caught me I was so lost in expectation,
frail with ecstatic longing while still I am awake and ah!—

'My friends, the god of the *cwm* is in his dragon-bone hall
within his fish-scale palace with its mother-of-pearl gates
and flinty rooms. Our shaman will meet him deep,
deep in the shallow water!'

>*I am your bride,*
>*I ride a white turtle,*
>*the striped fish follow,*
>*I offer myself to you*
>*in your many tributaries.*

'The ice is melting and our shaman is ready,
the god of the secret river when the storm comes
will travel in his flood, in his bright flush flood,
and they will meet for the great wedding.'

>*I am coming towards you, towards the west,*
>*I shall escort you to the shining blue bay,*
>*your trickles will become wild rolling waves,*
>*your waves will carry us on, I am your bride,*
>*great shoals of crimson fish are my bridal chorus.*

9. THE SECRET WOMAN OF CLEE HILL IS HIDING AGAIN

I know someone is there in that fold of the rocks.

'My friends, our shaman is climbing Clee Hill,
keep up your drumming, keep up your flute calls,
keep up your voice-strength.'

You are dressed in straggling creepers, in a belt of mistletoe,
you are watching me climb towards you, you are smiling,
inwardly saying 'I want you, I want you! Don't I please you?'

The Secret Woman of Clee Hill drives red foxes,
she leads striped wild cats, her chariot is made of heather

with banners of sheep's wool, her coat is of coarse flint,
her belt of ferns.

      Secretly are you picking sweet herbs
with which to return my love? I have come from my alder hut
where it is dark and I can't see the sky, I have climbed the hill
where the bright light hurts my eyes.

          'Now our shaman
is at the top of the mountain, dark clouds all around him.'

Even here now I can't see, even your *home is grim and gloomy.*

 'The west wind is blowing and blowing,
  our shaman needs courage,
  fierce rain is being sent by the Spirits
  protecting the Secret Woman of Clee Hill.
  Keep up your drumming! Keep up your flute calls!
  Keep up your voice-strength!'

Where can I find flowers here for her?
I shall have to make do with mushrooms and pieces of moss
that cover the boulders. If only I knew where she is.

 'Keep up your drumming!
  Keep up your flute calls!
  Keep up your voice-strength!'

I am sure the Secret Woman of Clee Hill wants to meet me.
Hasn't she led me, hasn't she led me here into the clouds?
I feel now so hurt I long only for my alder hut.

 'Keep up your drumming!
  Keep up your voice-strength!'

        O Secret Woman of Clee Hill,
you are wonderfully fragrant with the perfume of henbane!
I wish you smelt of wild onion and would sing storm.

 'Keep up your drumming!
  Keep up your flute calls!'

You drink from the mountain spring
and you become the spring itself,
you shelter under the beech trees
and you are their beauty.
I know you are thinking about me.
I know you are only holding back, shyly.

'Keep up your drumming!
Keep up your flute calls!
Keep up your voice-strength!'

Her chariot thunders away, the air is gruesome with rain,
the rabbits think it's a great joke, the wind whines,
the beeches shake. What have I got for my efforts
but to be stuck here alone and sad?

NOTE

These versions of the 3rd Century BCE Chinese *Nine Songs* were first stimulated, in 1993, by those of Arthur Waley (1955). I found also interpretative versions of one or two or all of the songs by David Hawkes, L. Cranmer-Byng and Burton Watson, and I read what I could about the songs' origins and meanings. Early on John Cayley responded very helpfully to my drafts, suggesting I try to bring out more strongly their ritual nature, and I have wanted to discover something of what the songs meant back then in China and what they might mean to us now, to which end I have used Welsh and West Midlands place-names. The first song is thought to be of a much later date and I have here truncated it.

NOTES

All Saints Elegies: Published in part in 'Leviathan' magazine and the whole in 'The Republic of Letters', Boston, USA, 2003. As I recall it, I responded poem by poem to Rilke's 'Duino Elegies', but as he wrote ten and I wrote thirty-three (some of them pruned now), something else must also have been happening. I live in All Saints Road.

TOWARDS THE LINE: ONE

A dance in two seasons: Published in 'Hand in Hand' (Picador, 2001), edited by Carol Ann Duffy.

On Athos, in the cafe at Daphni: The poem is whimsy mixed with memory. I had spent a week or so on Athos somewhere around the mid-1960s.

Soup of the Day: Written at the Dean Gallery, National Gallery of Modern Art, Edinburgh, June 2005, following my week in Poland.

The smell of death: In memory of my father.

Repeats: Published in 'Poetry Wales'.

Mr Amichai: Published in 'Lodestones', edited by Roger Garfitt (Border Poets, 2001). The Border Poets met for workshops at Walcot Hall, Shropshire, and this book published our poems 'written in celebration of twelve poets from around the world'. The sessions were led by Roger Garfitt and other members of the group. I led the one on Yehuda Amichai, and it happened that he had died—as also had R. S. Thomas—very shortly before.

Walking the streets of the boarded-up world: In 'Poetry Wales'.

I live in David's House: In 'Smiths Knoll', 2005.

Don't bark at me: In 'Lodestones'.

This is how it was: During a short residency based at Bronglais Hospital, Aberystwyth, 2003, I met by chance Fred Davies. We had not met before but when we began to share memories, they overlapped. Published in 'The Cambrian News'.

Work, the work Published as a Flarestack pamphlet, 2005. The poem was worked on over several years with radical shifts, cuts, rewritings taking in the reading of Beethoven's letters and notebooks and books concerned with his life and music. The sequence began as an attempt to inhabit Beethoven's final piano sonata, No. 32 op III. I don't play the piano but have long felt I make poems because I am unable to play music or compose. In my late teens that path began to be consciously not travelled, so I've been a long time aching. Towards the making of the poem, I listened to as many recordings of the sonata as I could find, began to take in the other late sonatas, and couldn't but notice that he was composing also the Missa Solemnis. A crucial moment was when Peter Spilsbury played through op.111 for me at his home in Moseley, Birmingham, played through it twice, re-played parts of it and responded to my questions. No recording by however illustrious a pianist can match the living thing. I'm grateful to Peter and of course to all the CD performers.

TOWARDS THE LINE: TWO

And following them: Runner-up, Cardiff International Poetry Competition 2005.

Borrow these: Commissioned by Poetry on Loan and published in its promotional brochure.

I think every day: A first draft was written at a monthly staff workshop at Heartlands Hospital during my residency.

He ran for them: Runner-up, Leviathan Competition 2003.

The manuscripts: Runner-up, Housman Competition, 2002.

Despair, Queuing with Trakl, and *Here's Gary Snyder on film*: In 'Lodestones'.

She's gone to Minehead: My note at the time says I wrote it 'during an event at *mac* (in Birmingham), in response to a photo. I'd gone to the loo and as I came out, two woman passed & one said to the other, 'She's gone to Minehead this week,' so I went back to the exhibitions looking for who it was had gone, and decided it was the woman in the portrait by Andreas Scholz & Tillmann Franzen, untitled.

The ward now coming into land: Poems and transcriptions from a residency with South Birmingham Mental Health NHS Trust 2000-2001. Poems and notes from the residency have been published in medical and poetry magazines, including 'Poetry Wales', 'Medical Humanities (Journal of Medical Ethics)' and 'Holistic Health'. For the song for the deaf, I am pleased to recall that Dave Newnham put my words to music and Nick Macartney gave the song studio backing and put it on to a CD. The sequence here is a revision of a presentation I gave at the 2005 Annual Conference of the Royal College of Psychiatrists in Edinburgh.

Corridors, stairs, lifts: Heartlands General Hospital, Birmingham. My own poems and those by staff were published in the hospital magazine, on banners and walls, and read aloud, during my time as Poet in Residence in the early 2000s, the residency relating primarily to staff but poems went also their own ways.

Song of the Mapmaker: A libretto of poems in response to the Hereford Mappa Mundi, with music by David Ventura, for tenor (some sections spoken, some sung), choruses and orchestra, performed in Hereford Cathedral 1998 and put on to CD. For the section 7 French translation I am grateful to Elizabeth Burridge. The late thirteenth-century map was made in Lincoln (with its 'smiling angel choir') and taken to Hereford.

TOWARDS THE LINE: THREE

The jigsaw of history has an infinite number of pieces: Written for the G8, Birmingham, issue of the annual 'Brummies All Write', 1998, titled 'Summit to write home about', edited by Dave Reeves, when I was Birmingham Poet Laureate 1997-98, and reprinted in the selected and final edition, 2000.

Scoffing cakes: Located at Manchester Cathedral following the first presentation of the cathedral poetry prize, for which I was the judge, 1999.

Eating chips with the saints: Commissioned and published by the Royal Mail for its presentation pack of Christmas stamps during the year of the Millennium. The subjects of the stamps were the lottery-funded newly built part of St Edmundsbury Cathedral, the Mystery Plays at York, the floodlighting of churches, and the proposed visitor centre at Downpatrick, which is where the poem began to be written, at the tomb, as it is said, of Patrick, Columba and Bridget.

Then in the twentieth century: Second prize, National Poetry Competition, published in the 'Independent on Sunday' and in 'Poetry Review', 2003.

Till receipt: Written as an irrefutable poem. In fact while till receipts after paying with a card are proof of purchase, a cash receipt could be picked up in the street. But believe me.

Here: Begun in the pulpit of the empty church at Aberdaron, where R. S. Thomas had once been Vicar. The poem is on sale as a card in that church.

Ten best benches, 2002 and *Ten best doors, 2003*: Invited by Stride and published on its web site.

Crossing: Written for and presented to Roy Fisher on the occasion of his becoming Honorary Poet of the City of Birmingham, 2003.

Itch, cram, britch and ratch: From poems of Birmingham, written — with Julie Boden's poems and Richard Green's photographs — for performance and exhibition in various Birmingham venues 2004. Plus a *Spaghetti Junction* poem commissioned along with those by other Birmingham poets and broadcast by Radio 3, 2002, and a *double acrostic* commissioned and published by 'The Independent' newspaper, 2004. For *Birmingham & the Black Country industry* I am indebted to Peter Wood's 'Industrial Britain: The West Midlands', 1976.

Haydn comes to lunch and sends a letter home: The Coull Quartet, resident at Warwick University, played Haydn's Opus 33 No. 2 in the Philosophy Department common room, at lunchtime, March 2002. 'Poetry uses up transcendence' is from Julia Kristeva, 'Desire in Language'. In the forest Paul Celan and Martin Heidegger. Spike Milligan died, as I recall, that same day.

It's in my soul, this: Written while Aldeburgh Poetry Festival Poet in Residence, 2001, with my photographs.

TOWARDS THE LINE: FOUR

Cædmon's song and a translation: Cædmon died in about 680 and this Anglo-Saxon poem is reckoned the first in English. The translation (based on other versions and my own work with a dictionary) was made during my residency at Worcester Cathedral 1997-8.

Went for a walk: Commissioned by the City of Birmingham Choir and spoken in Symphony Hall as part of a reading on the eve of Remembrance Day 2004, prior to a performance of Benjamin Britten's War Requiem.

Exile: Published as a part of the promotion of the Southwell Poetry Festival, when I was Poet in Residence.

The stiltwalkers: Written originally, in a form longer and more complex, during a course on which I was given a place at the Arvon Lumb Bank centre, on writing for radio. Later I was allocated funding to work on it. It found no place on radio, however, and instead went through many revisions as a poem.

After the party: 'The Path from the Year's Height', Border Poets, edited by Roger Garfitt, 1999.

The stone says: Written in Suffolk when I was Aldeburgh Poetry Festival Poet in Residence, 2001.

Given: Written at Thorpeness during a Poetry Trust course I was leading with Gillian Allnutt, September 2005.

Feldman says, if anyone asks: Runner up, Scintilla long poem competition 2004, and published in that journal 2005. While this poem found words for a long-time concern, I was moved towards it also by the book, 'Rodinsky's Room' (in the Princelet Street, Spitalfields, synagogue) by Rachel Lichtenstein and Iain Sinclair, and by individual visual images I found elsewhere. The numbering of the sections does not imply that any others are extant. For the latest on the use of the building see www.19princeletstreet.org.uk.

Felice-Grete: A libretto in search of a composer.

In the wings of the bones – A week in Poland: Runner up, Scintilla long poem competition 2005. During June, 2005, I spent a week with my daughter Cressy in Poland, from which came this sequence.

TOWARDS THE LINE: FIVE
Poems 2005–6.
Fine Line: Commissioned for use in West Midlands libraries.

Nine Songs: Published by Flarestack 1998 and performed in March of that year by voices and drums at Redditch Library. The version here is much revised. The image is from the original cover by Sally Delany for which again thanks.

Some poems have been revised following previous publication.

I am grateful to the many people with whom I've been lucky enough to work during these recent years. They know who they are. Sharing each other's writings over tea with Myra Connell has been important to me. The responses of Lizzi Thistlethwayte and Meredith Andrea to some of these poems have made a welcome difference. Charles Johnson has by his own work and his Flarestack publishing kept me believing that less obvious sense makes better sense. And Glenn Storhaug maintains his Five Seasons Press as something very special.

BIOGRAPHICAL NOTE

David Hart was born and grew up in Aberystwyth, Wales, was a
student in London and began work there as an Anglican priest. In
Birmingham, where he now lives, he worked first as a university
chaplain, later as a theatre critic and then arts administrator. He is again
now a freelance writer. He has held poetry residencies at Worcester
Cathedral (1998-9, where his open workshops continued until 2006),
South Birmingham Mental Health NHS Trust, Heartlands Hospital
(Birmingham), Bronglais Hospital (Aberystwyth), and the Aldeburgh
and Southwell Poetry Festivals. His Mappa Mundi-based *Song of the
Mapmaker* with music by David Ventura was performed in Hereford
Cathedral and is on CD. He created the Hay-on-Wye-Festival *Poetry
Squantum* and the West Midlands free magazine, *People to People*
(now *Raw Edge*, edited by Dave Reeves). His poems in response to
Georges Rouault's *Miserere et Guerre* were commissioned by and
exhibited at the Birmingham Museum & Art Gallery. Among many
prizes he has won 1st and 2nd in the National Poetry Competition.
He is currently an Honorary Teaching Fellow on the Writing
Programme at Warwick University, and at Birmingham University
a part-time Lecturer in Lifelong Learning. He was Birmingham Poet
Laureate 1997-8. His poems have been widely published in magazines
and anthologies, and in book form: *Setting the Poem to Words*, *Crag
Inspector: a poem of Bardsey Island* (both Five Seasons Press), and a
recent pamphlet long poem, *Work, the work* (Flarestack), starting
from an engagement with Beethoven's final piano sonata, which is
included in the present book.

PAPER SPECIFICATION / POLEMIC

The Five Seasons 'Original' recycled paper (110 gsm) used for this book is manufactured from one hundred per cent pre-consumer RCF (recovered fibre) sourced from scrap chiefly generated during printing and converting operations in the UK, with some addition of 'mill broke'.

No post-consumer fibre has been specified for this paper. This is because no paper mill in the UK currently manufactures quality recycled publishing papers using UK-sourced post-consumer fibre. Some all- or part-recycled publishing papers made in the UK *do* use MDIP (a market de-inked pulp made from post-consumer paper) but this is *imported*—principally from the USA and to a lesser extent from France. Publishers are being encouraged by various campaigns to specify post-consumer recovered fibre in UK-manufactured book papers but this is *not* reducing the amount of waste printed paper dumped in British landfill sites. The production of these 'environmentally-friendly' papers depends on long-distance pulp shipments.

The Waste & Resources Action Programme (WRAP — www.wrap.org.uk) published a major report in January 2005 on the feasibility of resolving this problem by building a pulp mill in the UK capable of producing the required post-consumer RCF pulp: *Market De-Inked Pulp Facility Pre-Feasibility Study* (ISBN 1-84405-142-0). Its findings suggest that a British MDIP facility is unlikely to be built in the near future because of various economic factors (and no British paper mill 'in the printings and writings sector' has 'shown an immediate interest in direct investment in the proposed MDIP plant').

So for the present Five Seasons Press has decided that the best policy is to promote awareness of this regrettable situation and to continue to use UK pre-consumer RCF rather than US post-consumer RCF in Five Seasons recycled papers. Five Seasons also prefers to specify a one hundred per cent furnish of these locally-recovered fibres rather than combine them with Forest Stewardship Council virgin fibres that, as likely as not, come from Uruguayan eucalyptus pulped in Morocco. Five Seasons Press agrees with WRAP's argument that the promotion of recycled paper *per se* is the critical issue. Improved facilities and options will only become economically viable when the demand for recycled papers (whether pre-consumer or post-consumer) increases.

It is of course much more difficult for a large publishing house than for Five Seasons to specify paper of this quality and (relative) probity. One of the many benefits of small-scale publishing.

Glenn Storhaug, publisher